Historic Gardens
of the Vale of Glamorgan

Edited by Hilary M. Thomas

Published by

Welsh Historic Gardens Trust

Ymddiriedolaeth Gerddi Hanesyddol Cymru

South and Mid Glamorgan Branch

ISBN-978-0-9558021-0-2

Contents

Endpapers: The Vale of Glamorgan, from George Yates's map of Glamorgan 1799.

Acknowledgements

Many individuals and institutions have helped in the production of this book, and it is a pleasure to record warm thanks to them all.

Especial thanks are due to the following who gave generously of their time and unique knowledge of family homes and gardens without which the book would have been immeasurably the poorer: Sue and David Beer; Sir Brooke Boothby; Sylvia Crawshay; Roddy Llewellyn; Jenny and Murray McLaggan; Carol and John Phillips; William Prichard; Lt.Col. Rhodri Traherne; Caroline, Lady Rhys Williams; Jennifer and Eric Williams.

The help and guidance given by members of staff in the following institutions is also acknowledged with gratitude: Glamorgan Record Office, Cardiff; Royal Institute of British Architects; Society of Antiquaries of London; Royal Horticultural Society, Lindley Library; Cadw/Welsh Historic Monuments; Royal Commisssion on the Ancient and Historical Monuments of Wales; Cardiff Central Library; Dyffryn Gardens & Arboretum, Vale of Glamorgan Council (with thanks to Gerry Donovan); Countryside & Environmental Projects, Vale of Glamorgan Council (with thanks to Chris Jones-Jenkins); Valeways; and the Glamorgan Heritage Coast Centre, Vale of Glamorgan Council (with thanks to Paul Dunn).

Many of the illustrations in the book have been provided by the above mentioned individuals and institutions and their source is duly acknowledged. Unacknowledged illustrations are from the editor's own collection. The drawings of fruit and flowers which appear on some of the pages, and which were commissioned especially for this publication, are the work of the botanic artist Gillian Griffiths.

A publication on historic gardens of the Vale of Glamorgan was first proposed by the Chairman and Committee of the South and Mid Glamorgan Branch of the Welsh Historic Gardens Trust whose support throughout the project has been greatly appreciated. Donald Moore gave wise counsel at various stages as the book progressed, and to him and to the many friends, too many to name individually, who gave continuing encouragement and advice, we are greatly indebted. Branch funds have contributed towards this publication. Financial assistance from the central committee of WHGT is gratefully acknowledged, as is a grant from the Ethel & Gwynne Morgan Charitable Trust.

This has been a collaborative project with each contributor bringing specialist knowledge and a personal perspective to individual gardens. We have endeavoured, in words and pictures, to share our enjoyment of and fascination with Glamorgan's historic gardens. Our readers will decide if we have succeeded in those endeavours.

The Contributors

(Autobiographical notes)

Hilary M. Thomas

Hilary Thomas was formerly a senior archivist in the Glamorgan Record Office. She is Joint Editor of *Morgannwg* (the journal of the Glamorgan History Society), a past President of the South Wales Record Society and an active member of the South and Mid Glamorgan Branch of the Welsh Historic Gardens Trust.

Brian Ll. James

Brian James was formerly Keeper of the Salisbury Library, University College, Cardiff. He has been Joint Editor of *Morgannwg* (the journal of the Glamorgan History Society) and General Editor of the South Wales Record Society.

Murray A. McLaggan

Murray McLaggan lived at Merthyr Mawr House from 1967 to 2005 with his wife Jenny (née Nicholl) and family. Over those forty or so years he observed the Merthyr Mawr gardens from the seat of his mower for about 10,000 hours. Much of the recent planting in the gardens has been the inspiration and work of his wife.

Derrick C. Kingham

Derrick Kingham was formerly Administrator of the Talygarn Miners' Rehabilitation Centre. He still lives within the Talygarn Registered Historic Garden and has a detailed knowledge of Talygarn House and the Clark family. He is a trustee of the Welsh Historic Gardens Trust and of the Cowbridge Physic Garden Trust.

Jeff Alden

Jeff Alden's particular interest was in the local history of Cowbridge and Llanblethian. He was Chairman of Cowbridge and District Local History Society, Editor of the Cowbridge Record Society, a member of the Council of the Glamorgan History Society and Treasurer of the Glamorgan County History Trust.
[Sadly, Jeff died before this book was published. ed.]

Foreword

Wales, with its temperate climate and varied topography, has many hundreds of beautiful and historic gardens, although only a select few are well known beyond the borders of the Principality. Bodnant, in north Wales, Powis Castle in Montgomeryshire, and, more recently, the National Botanic Garden of Wales in Carmarthenshire, attract many thousands of visitors each year, the vast majority unaware of the garden treasures which remain to be discovered by them in other parts of Wales. This is particularly true of the delightful Vale of Glamorgan area, the subject of Hilary Thomas's fascinating book.

Here are described, and copiously illustrated, great Edwardian gardens such as Duffryn and St Fagans Castle, which should be celebrated by a much wider audience, alongside little known but often important private gardens ranging in date from the Tudor period to the twentieth century. There are hidden gardens, rare survivors from past centuries; and lost gardens whose former glory has been erased from the landscape. And, as integral elements in the garden history of the Vale, the town gardens of Cowbridge and village gardens in Llanblethian and St Hilary are also featured.

Information on many of the gardens in this book has been brought to light as the result of new research by the contributors. Each garden has its own story to tell, and in many cases that story, intertwined as it is with people, events and social change, is revealed for the first time.

With the increasing interest in gardens and their history, this book will appeal not only to the general reader but also to the more informed garden visitor and dedicated garden historian. It fills an obvious gap in our knowledge of this important area and no doubt will become the essential reference work on Historic Gardens of the Vale of Glamorgan.

Dan Clayton Jones
Chairman (2003-2007)
Welsh Historic Gardens Trust, South and Mid Glamorgan Branch.

Access

Not all the gardens described in this publication are open to the public. Some are in private ownership and no automatic right of access can be presumed. Some allow regular access, some have occasional open days. The conditions of access are specified at the end of each entry.

Note on Sources

Primary and secondary sources specific to individual gardens are cited at the end of each chapter. A general bibliography of printed works relevant to Glamorgan gardens is included at the end of the volume (pages 244-5), and works cited here are referenced by short titles in the individual gardens' list of sources under 'see also'.

Watercolour sketches by Charlotte Louisa Traherne (née Talbot) illustrate some of the gardens described in this book. As not all the sketches can be precisely dated to years before or after the artist's marriage to the Revd J.M. Traherne in 1830 her married name is used in each caption.

Ash Hall, Ystradowen

The house stands on a south-facing slope above the village of Ystradowen towards the northern edge of the Vale of Glamorgan. It is a site which commands extensive views but which is also very exposed to the prevailing south-westerly winds, a combination which has had a major influence upon the form and content of the gardens attaching to the house.

The first garden at Ash Hall is believed to have been created by Matthew Deere early in the eighteenth century. Deere was a member of an emergent minor gentry family and is credited with having built the first house on the site. Long resident in Glamorgan, the socially ambitious Deeres numbered among their ranks attorneys, agents and clerics as well as farmers and were, by the beginning of the eighteenth century, possessed of considerable wealth. A member of the Rhoose branch of the family, Matthew Deere evidently shared that family's ambition for self advancement, acquiring an extensive, if scattered, landed estate comprising fifteen farms in the Vale and in the hinterland of Glamorgan. A landed estate demanded a seat for its owner and Ash Hall provided Deere with that symbol of prosperity and status.

Having achieved his ambition, Matthew Deere engaged the land surveyor and philomath William Jones to survey and map his property. Jones's map of the Ash Hall demesne, dated 1745, shows a four-square house of modest proportions with a central doorway, a regular pattern of fenestration and three large chimneys. It is a house only marginally grander than some of the farmhouses on other parts of Deere's estate, but set within its gardens it is clearly a property belonging to a 'gentleman'.

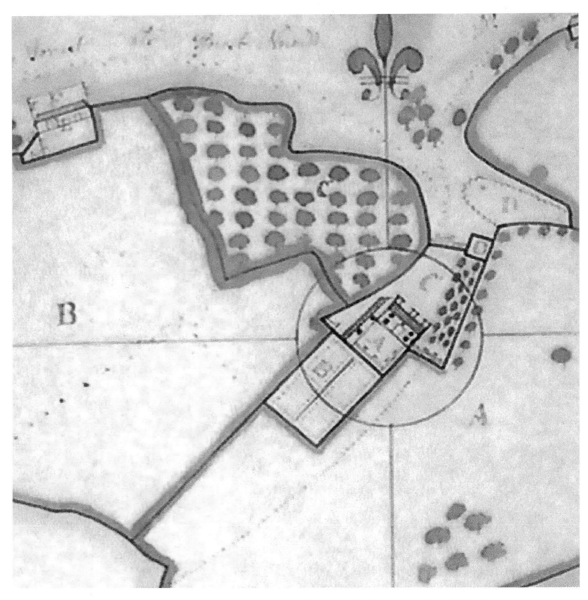

Above: Detail (enlarged) from Ash Hall estate map showing house and gardens, 1745 (Glamorgan Record Office).

Above: Ash Hall, photograph by Edwin Miles, early C20th (Glamorgan Record Office).

The gardens as shown on the 1745 map comprised three small enclosures, namely the Green Court, the Flower Garden and the Kitchen Court. The Green Court lay immediately in front of the house and seems to have been bounded on its east and south sides by walls ('stone fences') each with a pair of centrally sited pillars flanking a gateway. The protection of walls and hedges was essential on this exposed site and these features dictated the form of the Ash Hall gardens. The south gate of the Green Court, which on the map shows no paths or borders and was, presumably, an area of lawn, led into the Flower Garden which was laid out with geometric precision into four rectangles each contained within a hedge or bank. The Kitchen Court ran north of the house and was bounded on its eastern edge by a narrow plantation forming a shelter belt with perimeter walls giving protection to the site.

The main drive leading to the house was bordered by trees, and the massive sweet chestnut trees which survive today are undoubtedly survivors from the original planting.

This was an 'old fashioned' garden of formal design and small enclosures, created at a time when the vogue for the extensive landscape park was gathering momentum. The very location of Ash Hall on its elevated platform

Above: The Kitchen Garden, 2001.

ensured that the wider landscape, while physically excluded from the gardens, provided a constant panorama from the house, and the strategically placed clumps of trees shown on William Jones's map may indicate that some rudimentary 'landscaping' had taken place on the sloping ground below the house to the south.

If Matthew Deere was responsible for laying out the gardens at Ash Hall, it was his successor there, Colonel Richard Aubrey, a younger son of the Aubreys of Llantrithyd who improved them. Writing at the turn of the century, Benjamin Heath Malkin complimented the colonel on bringing his grounds into 'a state of cultivation and beauty far beyond what they possessed when I first knew them, by the judicious application of moderate labour and expense ...'. Malkin makes the interesting observation that Aubrey had 'disencumbered the lawn ... of those stone fences, by which it was formerly the custom of this county to shut out the beauties of the surrounding scenery'. The aesthetic, it seems, had triumphed over the practical. Stone from the 'fences' demolished by Aubrey may have been used to construct the ha-ha which still survives at Ash Hall today but of which the 1745 map gives no indication.

Above: Ash Hall in its setting, 2004.

One 'improvement' to which Malkin makes no reference concerns the kitchen garden. An eighteenth-century landscape garden was, essentially, green in concept. Flower and vegetable gardens were not allowed to intrude their colourful contents into the verdant panorama and were tucked away discreetly at some distance from the house, often behind stone walls. The walled kitchen garden at Ash Hall admirably meets these criteria, hidden as it is from the house, glimpsed but briefly from the drive. But its location is not that of the Kitchen Court shown on the 1745 map and this suggests that it was part of Richard Aubrey's improvements before his death in 1805.

Soon after this date the ornamental grounds at Ash Hall were described as 'displaying to the highest advantage the taste of the proprietor' and, as a succession of would-be owners and tenants viewed the property during the nineteenth century, their attention was drawn to gardens 'abundant and prolific beyond measure' and to the ornamental and protective plantations around the house.

Of the trees and shrubs with which the grounds were stocked at this period there is little surviving evidence, but a note made in 1850 reveals that the fruit trees included apple, plum, cherry and damson, an unexceptional and unnamed collection of which one or two venerable apples may still survive in the walled kitchen garden.

*Above: Trunk of
Sweet Chestnut tree
alongside the drive,
2001.*

*Below: Sweet Chestnut
tree, 2007.*

Today, at the beginning of the twenty-first century, elements of a 'Brownian' type landscape can still be discerned at Ash Hall: the green lawn on the south side of the house, from which there opens out the vista of the Vale with strategically planted individual trees and clumps leading the eye towards the parish church and medieval motte in the middle distance. It is a landscape in which nature and the hand of man have combined, fortuitously, to embrace the Natural, the Picturesque, and the Romantic.

Still visible at the foot of the slope are the remains of stone walls which formerly defined the southern boundary of the parkland, and a pair of stone gate-pillars. The pillars suggest an imposing carriage driveway giving access to the house, but the slope is far too steep to be negotiated by carriages, and the pillars while suggesting grandeur straddled but a footpath. Viewed from the south the whole prospect is framed by trees and bushes, among them a few mature Scots pines which, like the sweet chestnuts, were another long-lived species favoured by landscapers of parkland. It is likely that these were first planted at Ash Hall by Richard Aubrey to mark the boundary of the estate. Evidence from the Ordnance Survey maps of the late-nineteenth century suggests that, while many of these trees survived until the 1880s, by the end of the century a large number had disappeared from the landscape.

In 1866 Ash Hall became the residence of the self-made businessman Daniel Owen and remained in possession of the Owen family until the 1920s. Subtle changes to the gardens during that period are indicated on a succession of Ordnance Survey maps, most noticeably the erection of glasshouses south of the walled kitchen garden and the creation of what may have been a water or bog garden in an adjacent enclosure. Only the foundations and brick walls of the former

Above: Immature Sweet Chestnuts.

now survive together with some of the pipework of the heating and water installations, while the 'water garden' is overgrown and devoid of the wooden bridge which is said to have led to a central island.

Mrs Nancy Aston (née Owen), one of the last members of the Owen family to have lived at Ash Hall, recalled in her old age the gardens of her childhood in the early years of the twentieth century – the rose garden, the croquet lawn, the shrubberies, and the kitchen garden with its abundant supplies of produce for the house. Photographs taken during the First World War, when Ash Hall was used by the military as a convalescent hospital, show a profusion of roses climbing up the pillared verandah on the front of the house with a large monkey puzzle tree *(Araucaria araucana)* in the foreground. After the departure of the Owen family the gardens were neglected, in the words of Nancy Aston they were 'destroyed in favour of grassed areas for horses and greyhounds'. But the essential layout of the gardens survived and Nancy lived long enough to know that, in the hands of the present owners of Ash Hall, the work of reinstatement and restoration had begun.

Hilary M. Thomas

My husband John and I moved to Ash Hall with John's parents in 1967. The previous owners had divided the garden (with the exception of the front lawn) into paddocks for horses, and one of our first tasks was to open-up the garden by removing most of the fences.

Two gardeners were employed when we first came here – Mr Cruse who had previously gardened for my mother-in-law in Whitchurch, and Dai Maddy who had worked in the Ash Hall garden from the age of thirteen. Mr Cruse was a prize-winning vegetable gardener who worked mainly in the walled garden. Dai Maddy was also a great vegetable grower, notably of potatoes, and he too took great pride in the kitchen garden. I don't think there was much love lost between the two men! Dai Maddy finally retired when he was eighty-six years old, having given long and faithful service to Ash Hall, Monday to Friday every week. He was a great character, and I often think of

Above: Site of rose garden, 2007.

him in the garden, a shortish man with keen, twinkling blue eyes, his stick in his hand. He is buried in Ystradowen churchyard.

These two men kept the garden in good order throughout the late 1960s and the 1970s, during which period the rose garden was brought back to life producing glorious summer displays. But by the 1980s both men had died and we struggled to keep the gardens going. In 1992 we were fortunate to find someone who was very interested in the kitchen garden and who, for nine years, kept us supplied with fresh vegetables throughout the year and with sweet peas in the summer.

Below: Remains of glasshouses, 2007.

When we arrived at Ash Hall the walled garden contained old apple trees (four still survive but only two continue to yield fruit) and one pear tree (still producing fruit). We have planted apple and pear trees, a variety of soft fruit bushes and, more recently, vines, a peach tree and a pear tree to train against the south-facing wall.

Our present aim is to repair the walled areas of the garden and to retain as many original features as possible. In clearing away the weed and ivy from the walls of the old glasshouse behind the stables we have discovered that the fine quality bricks were all manufactured by the Pencoed brickworks. One of my long-term projects is to reinstate the water garden.

Carol Phillips

Private residence. No public right of access.

Sources

Primary
Map of the Ash Hall demesne by William Jones, 1745 (GRO D/DLI V/3 map1).
Ash Hall Estate Sale catalogue, 1840 (GRO D/DX207/1).
Secondary
Hilary M. Thomas, *Ystradowen, A Tale of Princes, Priests and People* (Ystradowen PCC, 1993).

Coedarhydyglyn, St George-super-Ely

T he first house called Coedriglan*, in the parish of St George-super-Ely, was built in 1767, but the name can be traced back more than two hundred years earlier when it was recorded as 'Reglines Wood' (1540). According to Rice Merrick 'Riglin' had once been a park, and while no other sources seem to confirm this it is worth remembering that Merrick lived at Cottrell, less than two miles away, and his statement can probably be relied upon. Coedriglan occupies steeply sloping and wooded ground in the southern part of the parish and manor, ground which may well have been reserved by the Flemings and Malefants, the late-medieval lords of St Georges and neighbouring Wenvoe, for hunting. Their manor house, now known as Castle Farm, a fifteenth-century building on an earlier fortified site, stands on the bank of the river Ely, the northern boundary of the parish.

The last of the Malefants died in the 1490s and the manor reverted to the chief lord of Glamorgan, thus becoming part of the Cardiff Castle estate until sold in the 1720s to Abraham Barbour, apparently a London lawyer. Barbour bequeathed his property to a local family of gentlemen farmers, the Llewellins, and from them there is an unbroken descent to the Trahernes who remain lords of the manor of St Georges today.

Abraham Barbour probably spent little time on his Glamorgan estate, but he did serve as sheriff of the county in 1725 when he was described as 'of St Georges' – so presumably Castle Farm was his 'seat'. Although we now consider Castle Farm a fine specimen of late-medieval domestic architecture, in the eighteenth century it must have seemed thoroughly old-fashioned

---

*The Coedarhydyglyn form of the name was adopted by Llewellyn Edmund Traherne around 1900, in the belief that it represented the supposed original meaning: 'wood along the valley'. For a full discussion of the forms of the name and its meaning, see G.O.Pierce, *Place-names in Glamorgan* (Cardiff, 2002), pp. 43-4.

A formal garden of lawns and beds was created close to the new mansion, the south lawn being partly cut into the slope, the lawn on the north and west sides sloping steeply. The topography of the site did not allow a really extensive formal garden and the main feature of the Coedriglan grounds then, as now, was its woodland, partly natural, partly planted. There seems to have been little development and change through Queen Victoria's reign until the Edwardian period when Llewellyn Edmund Traherne retired from the Navy and devoted himself to beautifying the garden at Coedriglan (henceforth Coedarhydyglyn). The Dell, a spring-fed narrow valley to the south of the house, was developed into a woodland and water garden in the Japanese fashion. A small stream was dammed to form a pool and a cascade, paths were made, exotic shrubs and other plants were introduced, a Japanese-style bridge and a wooden Japanese tea-house were constructed. The *Cardiff Times* journalist, who was shown around the house and grounds in 1911, was impressed by the way in which the natural setting had been enhanced, and not displaced, by horticulture. The *Register* notes the possible involvement of professional garden designers, the partners Parsons, Partridge and Tudway, at Coedarhydyglyn around 1905, but it is more likely that they worked at Bryngarw, north of Bridgend, for Captain Onslow Powell Traherne, a distant relative of Llewellyn Edmund Traherne.

Coedarhydyglyn remains in the possession of the Traherne family to the present day, each generation continuing the maintenance and enhancement of the park and garden landscape.

Brian Ll. James

Right: The Dell from the drive, 2006.

Left: The Glasshouse (now demolished) in the old walled Kitchen Garden (by kind permission of Rhodri Traherne).

Sir Cennydd Traherne and his wife Rowena, for long prominent figures in the public life of Glamorgan, took a special interest in the woodland surrounding their home at Coedarhydyglyn. The cypress garden and the pinetum which they planted are justly famous and won a number of prizes at the Royal Welsh Show. They were both members of the International Dendrology Society, but Lady Traherne was perhaps the more knowledgeable and enthusiastic, often displaying an encyclopaedic knowledge of her own conifers and impressing all around her by being able to recognise even the most obscure of species. It is true to say that, particularly during the 1960s and 1970s, few visitors to Coedarhydyglyn escaped without a visit to the pinetum, normally in the pouring rain! Sir Cennydd and his wife also planted a large number of interesting and rare rhododendrons throughout the woodland, which with the bluebells provide a colourful and spectacular start to the summer.

The gardens and woodland are now cared for by Sir Cennydd Traherne's nephew Rhodri and his wife Annabelle. They continue to plant and refurbish the Dell and have recently planted a large number of specimen conifers effectively joining up the cypress garden and the pinetum. Whilst Annabelle is happier planting, pruning, tidying and creating new vistas in the Dell or tending to her new kitchen garden, Rhodri has become fascinated by his trees. Indeed, he can often be seen late into the summer evenings with his two black Labradors in tow inspecting each and every one of his new conifers, checking that all is well and lavishing any tender loving care that may be necessary. There is little doubt that Lady Traherne would most certainly approve.

Rhodri Traherne

Right: In the Dell, 2006.

Private residence. No public right of access.

Sources

Primary
Tithe map and apportionment for St George-super-Ely, 1842-3 (GRO).
Information from Lieutenant Colonel Rhodri Traherne.
Secondary
C.F. Shepherd, *Local History: Sidelights on some Glamorgan Parishes* (Cardiff, 1946).
R.T.W. Denning, 'The Reverend John Montgomery Traherne', *Glamorgan Historian,* 4 (1967).
Cambrian, 13 February 1813.
Cardiff Times, 8 April 1911.

See also: Cadw/ICOMOS; Merrick; RCAHM(W), *Later Castles; Medieval Non-defensive Secular Monuments;* William Thomas.

The Court, St Fagans

The Court is now numbered among the many 'lost gardens' of
Glamorgan and its loss is significant, not because of any long history
but because of its association with one of the most influential figures
in garden design of the nineteenth and early twentieth century. That person
was Gertrude Jekyll and The Court was one of only five gardens in the whole
of Wales on which she is known to have been consulted. Artist, plants-
woman, author and garden designer, Gertrude Jekyll has been described as
'a gardener ahead of her time'. As a designer, she had a particular talent for
grouping plants in a way that combined dramatic effect with harmony of
colours, and her style of planting, particularly in hardy plant borders, created
an impression of natural informality. She collaborated with the eminent
architect and garden designer Sir Edwin Lutyens on many garden projects
and by the 1920s enjoyed a formidable reputation not only in this country
but also in Germany, Ireland and America. And it was in the 1920s that the
owners of The Court sought her advice.

The Court lies a short distance south of St Fagans Castle on the western edge
of Cardiff. The house was built early in the twentieth century for the chief
agent to the St Fagans estate, Robert Forrest, a date stone of 1907 over the
main entrance providing a precise building date. Robert Forrest died in 1910
and The Court was then occupied by the Cardiff shipping magnate William
Tatem (created Baron Glanely of St Fagans in 1918). In the 1920s The Court
was purchased by Sir David Llewellyn Bt. whose family home was Bwllfa,
Aberdare and whose wealth was derived from Glamorgan's coal resources.
His wife was Magdalena ('Madge') Harris and it was she who consulted
Gertrude Jekyll on the improvement and extension of the gardens at The
Court.

Lady Llewellyn's letters to Gertrude Jekyll provide detailed descriptions of the gardens as they were when the Llewellyn family moved into The Court. The overall layout of the grounds and much of the planting of trees and shrubs had been the work of the previous occupants and by the 1920s much of the planting was well established. A tree-lined sunken drive curved up to the house from the lodge on the west, climbing a slope which had been hollowed-out by earlier quarrying. The sides of the drive were heavily planted with rhododendrons and azaleas, while trees on the ridges above the drive included beech, silver birch and holly. Three fine cedar trees (two of them blue cedars) were a feature of the gardens. Narrow flower beds and plantings against the walls of the house, supplemented by plantings in tubs, dated from the Tatems' years at The Court. These were all considered 'too ostentatious' by Madge Llewellyn, were not favoured by Miss Jekyll and were swiftly removed.

As Lady Llewellyn's letters make clear, she was responsible for levelling the ground on top of the bank south of the drive to make a platform where 'a thatched wooden shelter' was erected, an octagonal structure known as 'the Wendy House', its weather vane depicting Peter Pan and Wendy. A rock garden was created on the north side of the platform, and on a knoll to the north of the drive was another wooden structure, a pavilion or 'Wembley Hut', reached by quarried stone steps, also the work of the Llewellyns. Below this slope lay the woodland garden, already well established by the 1920s. In these areas the advice of Miss Jekyll was sought on planting suitable varieties of roses, ground cover plants, shrubs to give colour and to screen the huts.

While seeking Gertrude Jekyll's advice on the planting and improvement of the existing garden, it was the area of lawn and field to the south of the house which offered the greatest scope for improvement and which Madge Llewellyn was determined to transform into an attractive garden. Since the arrival of the Llewellyns at The Court this area had provided the family with a cricket pitch, a tennis court and a riding area (the second son, Harry, would in adulthood win an Olympic equestrian gold medal at the Helsinki Olympic Games of 1952 on his horse Foxhunter). The cricket pitch on the eastern edge of the field would be retained, new tennis courts would be relocated and provided with a pavilion or 'garden house', and Miss Jekyll was involved in long discussions as to their overall setting and appropriate plantings to provide screening and edging. But Gertrude Jekyll's most significant input into the garden at The Court was the design and planting of the new extension immediately south of the house. From the consultations between the two

Below: The Gertrude Jekyll borders looking north towards the house, past the circular pond and sweet chestnut tree, c.1930 (by kind permisssion of Mrs David Prichard).

women there emerged two wide borders flanking a broad grass path and running south from the fine semi-circular yew hedge which separated the front croquet lawn from the wider lawn and field beyond. Enclosed by protective yew hedges, the borders vista centred on a mature sweet chestnut tree. A further extension agreed between Madge Llewellyn and Gertrude Jekyll comprised a sunken area with ponds, lavender-lined paved paths and roses. Planting within the borders began in January 1926 and was typically 'Jekyll' – long drifts of colour running from warm reds and oranges near the house to cool mauves and silvers in the distance. The whole concept must, when realised, have looked magnificent, a tribute to the two women who conceived it and to the gardeners who executed the designs.

Above: The Gertrude Jekyll borders looking east across the circular pond, c.1930 (by kind permisssion of Mrs David Prichard).

It is known that the work of constructing the rock garden and pools was entrusted to the firm of Gage's and that Mr Hibbert, an employee of that firm, was retained by Lady Llewellyn because her own resident head gardener, Mr Appleby, who lived in one of the lodges, was fully occupied in looking after the walled kitchen garden and the glasshouses. Heathers recommended by Miss Jekyll for planting around the new tennis courts were obtained from the Dorset firm of Maxwell and Beale, while the Somerset firm of Kelway supplied the plants for the herbaceous border on the east side of the north lawn, one area of the grounds on which Miss Jekyll was not consulted.

Sir David and Lady Llewellyn and their eight children derived enormous pleasure from the gardens. Madge Llewellyn, well-read on matters of gardening and possessed of a good knowledge of plants, had decided views on just what she wanted to achieve in the gardens at The Court, and she had the satisfaction of seeing the gardens transformed. Gertrude Jekyll, already in her eighties and with failing eyesight when she was first consulted by Madge Llewellyn, communicated all her designs and comments in correspondence and never visited St Fagans to see her scheme implemented. Sadly, neither the 'Jekyll garden' nor the wider gardens of The Court survived the century.

Right: The Rock Garden and pond, with Miss Elaine Llewellyn, 1930s (by kind permission of Mrs David Prichard).

Above: The Cowbridge Physic Garden, 2007 (Robert Moore).

The garden has been created as an amenity for Cowbridge and the wider community and also to provide an insight into the long history of plants as sources of medicines and of their present-day crucial role in pharmaceutical research.

The Grammar School

In Church Street, between the south gate and the church, stands the former Grammar School building. Established early in the seventeenth century, 'Cowbridge Free School' as it was originally known, occupied modest premises on the site of the building which now stands and which was rebuilt in Gothic style in the mid-nineteenth century to the designs of the Llandaff diocesan architect, John Prichard. Within the precincts of the new, larger buildings, and bounded on two sides by the town wall, was the headmaster's garden which, with its neat lawn, flower beds and raised banks, evoked the secluded garden of an Oxford college, an appropriate evocation in the light of the school's close connection with Jesus College, Oxford.

Right: The gardens at the old Free (Grammar) School as shown on a Nantgarw plate, c.1818/19 (National Museum Wales).

Right: The headmaster's garden, Cowbridge Grammar School, c.1970.

Richard Williams, headmaster from 1919 to 1938, who also described the Old Hall gardens, has left an affectionate and nostalgic picture of the school garden:

the unique lawn – a haven of peace undisturbed by the mad rush of soul-less motors along the main road, the fresh green of its grass enclosed by the storied ramparts of walled Cowbridge, with stately copper beeches and strong yet graceful ilex standing sentinel upon them, the gnarled and twisted medlar tree with now but a flicker left of the life that has sustained it 150 years or more, the bright splashes of the flowers that Penny's skill produces in profusion …

The headmaster's garden was abandoned when the old school building became disused; the hope is that it will soon be restored to some of its former beauty to complement the new apartments.

Dynevor Cottage see entry under **Llanblethian, village gardens**

Market Gardens in Cowbridge
Although each house in the town had its burgage plot, there seems to have been the need for commercial gardening; but it is difficult to determine how far back such a need was felt.

A deed of 1631 related to 'land called the hopiard containing five burgages'. The hopyard was at the west end of town (just before the Llantwit Major road branches off). It had been five burgage plots during the heyday of medieval Cowbridge, between 1250 and 1350, but after that the population markedly decreased and many houses – especially those along Westgate – fell into decay. It is not possible to say for how long hops were actually grown on this piece of land; it is generally accepted that hops were used to flavour beer only from the sixteenth century onwards. The name survived, but by the 1840s it was described as a meadow. 'Hopyard Meadow' is now a cul-de-sac of modern houses.

The first market garden as such is found mentioned in the burgage rentals from 1738 onwards as 'Early's Garden', Early being the man or family that worked it. One of his successors, Robert Arnot, was listed in the *Universal British Directory*, published in the 1790s, as 'Gardener and Seedsman'. Early's and Arnot's garden (reckoned at three quarters of an acre) was located at 11A Westgate, next to Broad Shoard. They also had a house and another large garden on the opposite side of the street, where the police station and nearby premises were later built. The gardeners would probably have sold their produce, seeds and plants from a stall on market day – there were no greengrocers' shops in Cowbridge until the very end of the nineteenth century. Arnot's successor, Robert Church, had the market garden on the police station site, but 'Early's Garden' seems to have ceased to be a market garden before the end of the eighteenth century, by which time it was let to the licensee of the Bear. In 1913 it is actually referred to in a sale catalogue as 'the Bear Garden', and as such it would have supplied Cowbridge's principal inn with vegetables and fruit.

There are no references to market gardening in Westgate later than the 1850s. Another market garden, behind 22 High Street, is mentioned above under the heading of Great House. Many residents of the town still remember Mr Bessant's much larger market garden in the angle between Broadway and the St Athan Road, where the Brookfield Park houses were built in the 1970s.

Brian Ll. James (with acknowledgement to JA and HMT)

*Old Hall gardens and Cowbridge Physic Garden
are open to the public throughout the year.*

Sources

Primary
Cowbridge tithe award, 1843 (GRO and NLW).
Edmondes Collection (GRO D/D Ed).
A Catalogue of the Household Furniture etc. of John Edmondes Esq., 1778 (D/D E689).
Diaries of Revd F.W .Edmondes (GRO).
Dunraven estate deeds (NLW).

Secondary
Peter Cobb, *At Cowbridge Grammar School 1949-1966* (Cowbridge Record Society, 2001).
Iolo Davies, '*A Certaine School': a History of the Grammar School at Cowbridge, Glamorgan* (Cowbridge, 1967).
Jeff Alden, *Cowbridge: Buildings and People* (Cowbridge Record Society, 1999).
David M. Robinson, *Cowbridge the Archaeology and Topography of a Small Market Town in the Vale of Glamorgan*
(Glamorgan-Gwent Archaeological Trust, 1980).
Jeff Alden (ed.), *Cowbridge and District Remembered 1900-1950* (Cowbridge Record Society, 2002).
Llantwit Major and Cowbridge: a Study of the Historic Domestic Architecture (Royal Commission on Ancient and Historical Monuments in Wales, 1989).

Craig-y-parc, Pentyrch

Craig-y-parc stands on a ridge south-west of the village of Pentyrch, a few miles north-west of Cardiff, and looks out across the Vale of Glamorgan. It is a striking example of a house and garden conceived as one complementary composition under the strong influence of the Arts and Crafts Movement. The architect and garden designer was C.E. Mallows (1864-1915), his client was Thomas Evans, director of the Ocean Coal Company, and the whole project was carried out between 1913 and 1918.

The house was built in a Tudor-vernacular style from stone quarried on site, with dressed Cotswold stone used for pillars and other details and with Cotswold stone roof tiles. The southern façade incorporates a colonnaded atrium which is open in its central portion giving immediate access down a wide flight of steps to the main area of the gardens which lie to the south on steeply sloping ground.

The central features of Mallows's formal, symmetrical design for the gardens to the south and west of the house are a series of terraces and lawns buttressed by low stone walls and linked by flights of stone steps and stone-paved paths. With its strong north-south axis centred on the house, the design provides for panoramic views across the Vale of Glamorgan to unfold beyond the gardens.

Below: South front of house, 2002.

The need, when designing a garden, to relate garden to house and the house and garden to the surrounding landscape was a philosophy shared by many of Mallows's contemporary landscape architects and designers, among then Sir Edwin Lutyens and Thomas Mawson (who in 1906 had designed the magnificent gardens at Duffryn for Reginald Cory). It is a philosophy which finds full expression at Craig-y-parc.

Right: Plan of the grounds by Charles Edward Mallows, 1913 (Royal Institute of British Architects).

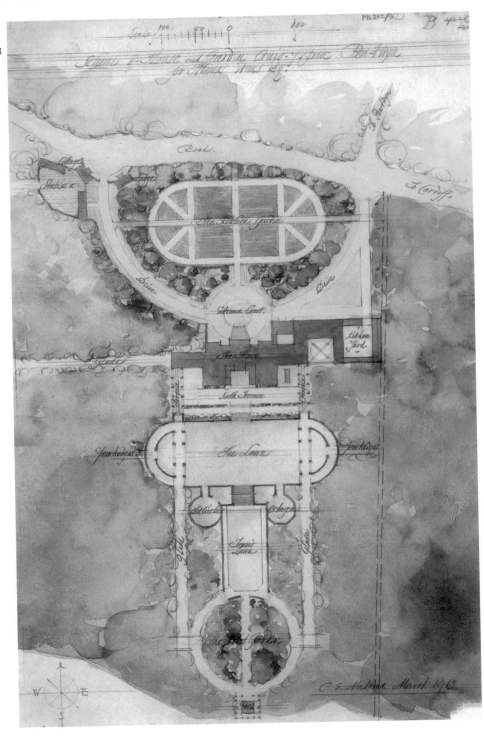

Above: South aspect from house, 2002.

Below: Balustrading, 2002.

Immediately outside the south front of the house is a long, stone-flagged terrace with a low parapet wall topped with balustrading. From the centre of this terrace broad flights of stone steps lead down through two narrow terraces to a level lawn bordered by yew hedges and with a semi-circular walled bed on its east side. Beyond and below the main area of lawn is a flagstone platform with side steps leading to a curving grassed terrace above a circular enclosure or 'amphitheatre' in parts of which the rock face is exposed. On the east side of the main gardens a series of narrow, flat grass terraces linked by flights of stone steps also lead down towards the amphitheatre. And on the uppermost terrace there survive two garden buildings typical of the Arts and Crafts Movement – an open-fronted loggia or garden pavilion and a rustic stone and wood hut above the amphitheatre.

Above: The Salmon Leaps.

Private residence. No public right of access. The Valeways 'Salmon Leaps' footpath walk affords good views of the Cwrtyrala cascades.

Sources

Primary
Michaelston-le-Pit tithe map, 1843 (GRO).

Secondary
Cardiff Times, 25 February 1911.
S.K. Jones, 'The manor of Michaelston, with particular references to Cwrtyrala and the Rous family', Diploma in Local History, Extra-mural Department, University College, Cardiff, 1981.
Marie Trevelyan, *Holiday Haunts in Glamorganshire* (Cardiff, 1899).
Chrystal Tilney, *Glimpses of Old Dinas Powys* (Risca, 1982).

See also: Cadw/ICOMOS; Malkin; Newman; Pierce; Royal Commission, *The Later Castles.*

Dimlands, Llantwit Major

D imlands lies on the southern edge of the Vale of Glamorgan between Llantwit Major and St Donats. Only two fields and a road separate it from the cliff top and the Bristol Channel, and while the site commands splendid views southward to the Devon and Somerset coast it is fully exposed to the prevailing winds. In all such locations, the design and layout of gardens will be determined in large measure by the need for protective walls, hedges and shelter belts.

Far Right: Detail (enlarged) from Dimlands estate map showing house and gardens, early C19th (Glamorgan Record Office).

The gardens at Dimlands were laid out soon after 1800 when the owner of the estate, the Reverend Robert Nicholl, a younger son of the Nicholl family of The Ham, Llantwit Major, built the first house there. A contemporary map of the property provides a precise picture not only of the design and proportions of the house but also of the layout of the gardens.

The house, a plain three-storey edifice with projecting single-storey wings, faced south across a small semi-circular enclosure, presumed to be a lawn, within a larger grassed area of some five acres. The main gardens to the north-east of the house lay within stone walls and were laid out in a formal pattern. This walled enclosure was divided into two rectangular areas each with clearly defined paths and geometric beds. Shrubberies and plantations lined the southern extremity of the Dimlands site, those on the west having a functional value as shelter belts (essential when the exposed nature of the site is considered), others with a more aesthetic purpose.

Dimlands provided a residence for members of the Nicholl family until *c.*1870 and during those years the gardens were carefully maintained. Records reveal that the Reverend Robert and his son John Whitlock Nicholl Carne took a keen interest in the gardens and, in particular, the planting of trees and the

Right: The Walled Garden, 1990s.

Bottom Right: Surviving stretch of walling, 1990s.

Bottom Left: Remains of gardeners' bothy, 1990s

Above: Francis Crawshay's stone chair.

In many ways these small-scale gardens attaching to a minor gentry property in the Vale of Glamorgan were unexceptional in layout or content. The Dimlands gardens reflect the taste, interests and resources of the Nicholl family in the nineteenth century, and much of their historic interest derives from the surviving documentation which places them within the lives and activities of that family's members.

Dimlands was sold in the 1950s when the old house was demolished and five modern houses were built on the site, each with its own area of land. On the wall of one of the modern houses is a much weathered stone slab bearing the Carne coat of arms (Robert Nicholl assumed the additional surname of Carne on his marriage to the Carne heiress) and a long, eulogistic inscription on the genealogy of the two families. This, together with the lodge which survives as a private residence, recalls the heyday of Dimlands. Today, the most obvious reminder of the Dimlands gardens is the walled kitchen garden, still intact with its two compartments, one now complete with swimming pool, one retaining the dilapidated remains of a small stone structure – the gardeners' hut or bothy indicated on the early nineteenth-century map. Elsewhere, only short stretches of old stone walls, some with arches and doorways, and the occasional 'ancient' tree survive to recall the lost gardens of Dimlands.

Hilary M. Thomas

Private residences. No public right of access.

Sources

Primary
Dimlands estate map, c.1800 (GRO D/DC E/46).

Secondary
Hilary M. Thomas, 'Dimlands, Llantwit Major. A Small-Scale Gentry House in Glamorgan', *Archaeologia Cambrensis* Vol.153, 2004 (publ. 2006).

Duffryn, St Nicholas

Duffryn, St Nich

The magnificent Edwardian gardens and arboretum at Duffryn* were the creation of the renowned landscape architect Thomas Mawson and the distinguished amateur horticulturalist Reginald Cory, owner of Duffryn. Created in the first decades of the twentieth century they are, without doubt 'the grandest and most outstanding Edwardian gardens in Wales'. Covering some 55 acres (22ha) the gardens and arboretum lie in a sheltered valley a short distance to the south of St Nicholas village and a few miles south-west of Cardiff.

In 1891 Duffryn was purchased by the wealthy ship owner, coal owner and philanthropist John Cory who built a grandiose new mansion on the site of an earlier house which had been home, successively since the sixteenth century, to generations of the Button, Pryce and Bruce families. The new mansion was constructed between 1893 and 1894 to the design of the Newport architect E.A. Lansdowne. The house is approached from the north via a porte-cochere which leads into a lofty hall boasting a superb marble chimneypiece with carved wood figures, and a huge stained glass window. Fine oak panelling and more marble and alabaster chimneypieces are features of the other main rooms. But impressive as was the house, it was the gardens which were to become Duffryn's enduring claim to fame.

The Ordnance Survey map of 1900 shows that Cory had, by then, made some changes to the parkland which had previously surrounded the house and had created a tennis-lawn and informal lake to the south. Old walled gardens to the west of the house, a legacy from previous owners, were retained.

*Historically, Duffryn was the spelling preferred by owners of the estate. Dyffryn is the form of the name used by the Vale of Glamorgan Council.

Above: Aerial View, 1999. (Dyffryn Gardens & Arboretum, Vale of Glamorgan Council).

Each of these 'garden rooms' (which pre-date the better-known examples at Hidcote in Gloucestershire and Sissinghurst in Kent) has its own character not only in design but also in planting and here, as elsewhere in the garden, Reginald Cory's deep knowledge of plants and his interest in garden design complemented Mawson's professional skills and guided the activities of the head gardener Mr Cobb.

From the Mediterranean Terrace a short flight of stone built steps leads via an archway into the Herbaceous Border which runs the full length of a south-west facing terrace and which is bounded on the north-west by the wall of the Kitchen Garden. Beyond the Herbaceous Border lie the garden rooms,

Left: The Italian Terrace [alias The Herbaceous Border] watercolour by Edith H. Adie, 1923 (RHS, Lindley Library).

Right: The Fountain Court [now designated The Pompeiian Garden], watercolour by Edith H. Adie, 1923 (RHS, Lindley Library).

Right: The Cloisters [now designated The Theatre Garden], showing Reginald Cory's collection of Bonsai, watercolour by Edith H. Adie, 1923 (RHS, Lindley Library).

Above: Pompeiian Garden, early C21st.

the secret gardens of Duffryn: the Cloister or Lavender Walk, the Theatre Garden, the Paved Court (whose design is credited to Cory) with its semicircular alcove, wall fountain and dipping pool below a balustraded terrace, the Bathing Pool Garden (now grassed) and the Round or Rose Garden also known as the Topiary Garden from the formally clipped box edgings which originally surrounded the rose beds. The Theatre Garden (alias the Japanese Garden) includes a stone paved dais built to display Cory's fine collection of bonsai trees and Japanese ornaments. The narrow compartment east of the Theatre Garden gives access to the Pompeiian Garden with its colonnades, loggias and fountain. Built in 1909 (and recently restored) this garden was modelled on gardens excavated at Pompeii.

An opening in the yew hedge of the Rose Garden affords a vista eastwards across the Great Lawn to the Arboretum where Cory planted a magnificently varied collection of trees, many of them species then of recent introduction into the British Isles. A Chinese paper bark maple *(Acer griseum)* was probably one of the original such trees brought into the country by E.H. 'Chinese' Wilson. This, together with other significant introductions including the pocket handkerchief tree *(Davidia involucrata)* and Brewer's spruce *(Picea breweriana)* are among Cory's most notable trees growing at Duffryn today.

An arboretum planned for the western edge of the grounds was never planted, but this informal area of lawns and woodland clearings, the West Garden, does contain many rare trees and shrubs. Also flourishing here is a white flowered wisteria *(Wisteria venusta)*, probably the one given to Cory by his friend Ellen Willmott, the renowned gardener, in 1916.

In the south-west corner of the grounds, beyond the garden rooms, a separate, enclosed garden was made for Cory's large-scale dahlia trials (Cory was President of the National Dahlia Society), trials which helped to restore the popularity of the dahlia as a decorative garden plant. This garden no longer survives. At the southern extremity of the West Garden and the Great Lawn, in a natural depression of the ground, Mawson and Cory planned to make a lake, with an observation tower and water pavilion. The lake project was abandoned when filling the lake caused flooding of the cellars in the house

Above: Dipping Pool, Paved Court, early C21st

and only the observation tower was built. A sale catalogue of 1937 refers to Water, Peony and Bog gardens on the site of the proposed lake but of these all sign has long vanished.

Below: The Paved Court, watercolour by Edith H. Adie, 1923 (RHS, Lindley Library).

Above: The Swimming Pool Garden, watercolour by Edith H. Adie, 1923 (RHS, Lindley Library).

Also at the southern extremity of the Great Lawn and adjacent to the proposed lake, are two more enclosed gardens: the Pool Garden (also called the Lavender Court) enclosed on two sides by brick-built arcading and on two by hedges and originally containing typically Edwardian white painted trellis, and the Heart Garden so named from its shape. This was probably the last area of the gardens to which Mawson devoted his attention, and with the outbreak of the First World War work at Duffryn faltered and ceased, to be resumed by Cory when peace was restored.

Between them, Thomas Mawson and Reginald Cory created magnificent gardens at Duffryn, and today those gardens are a living testimony to the skills and knowledge of both men. Mawson is remembered as an important landscape architect who worked in many parts of this country and abroad both on private gardens and public parks. Cory is highly regarded in horticultural and botanical circles for his profound knowledge of plants and their cultivation and particularly for his bequests to institutions such as the

Above: House (south front) from west, early C21st.

Royal Horticultural Society Lindley Library and the Cambridge University Botanic Garden. But it is the gardens at Duffryn which are, in many ways, his most enduring legacy. Here, his support of plant-hunting expeditions, his own travels in search of plants in the wild, his friendship with such luminaries of the botanical and horticultural world as Lawrence Johnston of Hidcote, Lionel de Rothschild and H.J. Elwes, and his contact with plant hunters such as E.H. Wilson and F.K. Ward are reflected in the rich variety of trees and plants which survive from his original plantings. The full glory of Duffryn in its heyday is revealed in paintings and photographs of the early twentieth century – the massed collections of lilies, the profusions of rambler roses, the swathes of wisteria against the south front of the house and the festoons of nasturtiums tumbling from the tops of the colonnades in the Pompeiian Garden. In the years since the Second World War financial constraints, and reductions in the number of gardening staff have influenced the maintenance and planting at Duffryn. Edwardian grandeur has, in many areas, given way to a more utilitarian landscape.

*Above: South front,
long vista, early C21st.*

Right: Seat and Urn.

Above: The Swimming Pool, still with white wisteria 2000.

Right: Statue and Topiary.

Above: The Rose Garden, 2000.

Below: Pool Garden/ Lavender Court with white painted trellis, temp. Cory (Glamorgan Record Office).

Right: Pool Garden/ Lavender Court restoration, 2006.

Above: Herbaceous Border, early C21st.

Now, at the beginning of the twenty-first century, with grants secured from the Heritage Lottery Fund, the gardens created by Mawson and Cory are being restored to their Edwardian splendour and their significance underlined.

Hilary M. Thomas

Gardens open to the public all year round.
Admission charges apply from April to October.

Sources

Primary
Sale Catalogue of the Dyffryn estate, 1937 (copy in GRO).
Watercolours of Duffryn house and gardens by Edith Helena Adie (1864-1947), c.1920 (Lindley Library, Royal Horticultural Society, London).
Photographs taken by Neame Roff, c.1920 (GRO, Cory album).

Secondary
Mawson, T., *The Art and Craft of Garden Making* (London, 1926).
Patricia Moore and Stephen Torode, *Duffryn, an Edwardian Garden Designed by Thomas H. Mawson* (GRO, 1993).
Stephen J. Torode, 'The Gardens at Duffryn, St Nicholas, Glamorgan. The Creation of Thomas Mawson and Reginald Cory', *Gerddi* Vol.III, 2000/2001.
Kay Sanecki, 'Reginald Cory, Botanist and Benefactor', *The Garden,* **118** part 2 (February 1993).
John Sales, 'Dyffryn, near Cardiff', *Country Life,* CLXXX (23 and 30 October 1986).
The Gardeners' Chronicle 12 December 1914, 3 July 1920 and 19 May 1934.
The Garden, Journal of the Royal Horticultural Society, Vol. 118 part 2, Feb.1993.
Cardiff Times, 7 October 1911.

See also: Cadw/ICOMOS; Royal Commission, *The Greater Houses.*

Dunraven Castle, St Brides Major

From the early nineteenth century until the mid twentieth century a large, castellated Gothic mansion dominated the north flank of Trwyn y Witch headland above Southerndown Bay and the Bristol Channel. Photographs of the house and grounds in their heyday reveal magnificent walled gardens, extensive parkland and plantations, and immaculately tended lawns. But in 1962 the house was demolished and today the remaining garden features are but a pale echo of their former glory.

The castellated mansion was built *c*.1803 for Thomas Wyndham MP on the site of a much earlier and less pretentious house which had been the ancient seat of the Vaughan and Butler families. The houses were built within the ramparts of a large Iron Age hillfort thereby destroying parts of the outer ramparts.

The Wyndham family, of Clearwell in Gloucestershire, acquired Dunraven in the seventeenth century but did not use the property as more than an occasional 'hunting' residence until the rebuilding by Thomas Wyndham, then owner of the combined Llanmihangel and Dunraven estate through the marriage of his grandfather with the Llanmihangel heiress Anne Edwin. Caroline Wyndham, only daughter and heiress of Thomas, married Windham Quin of Adare in Ireland and thence Dunraven passed into the possession of the earls of Dunraven.

The earliest known depictions of house and gardens are to be found in the watercolours and engravings of Francis Grose and Samuel Hooper and date from the 1770s. They reveal that the main elements of the later gardens were already in place, notably the perimeter wall of the deer park (probably of seventeenth-century origin) and the walled garden below and to the north-east of the house. Strong walls, fences and shelter belts were essential features in such an exposed site, serving not only to afford protection from the prevailing, salt-laden winds but also to keep the deer in the park well away from the pleasure gardens. The Grose/Hooper view shows that in the late-eighteenth century the walled garden was of irregular shape and that its walls were uncrenellated. Internally, at the east end of the garden, there appear to have been two low walls or banks which may have supported terraces. The perimeter wall of the park runs up to the top of the headland encircling, on the east, the ramparts of the Iron Age fort which the artist prominently indicates. Part of a walled enclosure is shown in the north-east corner of the view, within the perimeter wall.

Above: c.1950

Below: 2005

Left: Aerial views of the walled gardens (Glamorgan Heritage Coast Centre, Vale of Glamorgan Council).

The rebuilding of the house in 1803 and its subsequent extensions and improvements by members of the Dunraven family in the 1850s and 1880s were accompanied by improvements to the gardens. Drives were constructed, lodges built at the main drive entrances, the park was heavily planted with trees and a substantial crenellated stone wall was constructed around the park. The Earl of Dunraven, in his account of the castle written in the 1920s, states that 'the sea walks, so cleverly constructed along the side of the east cliff leading down to the Witches Point … were designed by the late Lord Dunraven about the year 1840'. The Grose/Hooper engravings suggest that at least some of these paths followed the lines of the ancient ramparts and owed their origins to an earlier 'landscape architect'. A few winding paths do still survive on the headland among the trees and bushes which cling tenaciously to the slope.

Below: Garden shelter, 2005.

Above:
Remains of glasshouses
with banded brickwork,
2005.

Below:
Palm tree in walled
garden.

The Ordnance Survey map of 1877 provides a detailed ground plan of the Dunraven gardens at that date. Some of the man-made features which then adorned the landscape have long since disappeared, among them the 'flagstaff', a circular feature on the headland, which itself seems to have replaced an earlier octagonal building shown on an 1830s view, and a fountain south of the walled garden. But the walled garden as shown on the map does survive, albeit as a skeleton, its walls denuded of glasshouses, its compartments retaining few of the exotic and other plants which once flourished there. High crenellated walls still surround the rectangular site which is divided laterally into three compartments which had both utilitarian and ornamental functions, providing fruit and vegetables to tempt the palates of the household and flowers, trees and shrubs to delight the senses. Within this sheltered environment the variety and profusion of plants was spectacular.

Today, despite the best efforts of the staff and volunteers at the Glamorgan Heritage Coast Centre, the gardens are starkly bare. Coloured bricks line walls where glasshouses once stood, there are a few bases of cold frames, a few ancient apple trees, a single ancient mulberry and, until recently, one venerable medlar, all survivors from a more affluent age. A niche in the north wall survives with water-worn rockwork, there is a paved area at the west end of the garden, some stone steps and a fireplace niche in the west wall denoting where a gardener's house once stood. The castellated structure in the south wall as shown in nineteenth-century photographs no longer stands but may be identified today with the derelict and largely collapsed structure in the central walled area. The internal dividing walls with their Tudor and arched doorways, the grassed terraces and borders, the perimeter and other paths edged with sea-polished stones, and the

Right:
Pebble edging to paths.

Right:
In the walled gardens,
2005.

circular stone-built pond in the western compartment all remain to recall the heyday of the gardens. And there are two features, in particular, which recall a former age: the Edwardian summerhouse with its red-tiled pitched roof on a terrace below the south-west wall looking out across a level lawn (probably once a croquet lawn or tennis court) to the terrace beyond; and the round stone tower in the south-east corner of the garden with its crenellated top and the Dunraven family coat of arms above the entrance. Built to provide a viewing room and banqueting room on its upper floor and an ice house below, this latter structure (restored in the 1980s) still dominates the garden landscape.

Above: Tower containing a banqueting room and an ice house.

Of the once imposing mansion 'Dunraven Castle' only few stone footings, short flights of steps and the revetment walls of the platform on which the house was built survive, alongside and above the Tudor arch under which the former north drive passed. But it is from the vantage point of the house platform that the full extent of the walled garden can best be appreciated.

Hilary M. Thomas

Gardens and parkland of 'Dunraven Park' open to the public free of charge throughout the year.

Sources

Primary
Dunraven estate map, by Edward Thomas, 1779 (GRO D/D Dun E/1 map1).
View of Dunraven by Francis Grose (ink & watercolour), c.1775; and engraving by S. Hooper after F. Grose, 1776.
Photographs of the gardens taken in the late C19th and early C20th.

Secondary
Earl of Dunraven, *Dunraven Castle* (1926).
Hopkins, T.J., 'Francis Grose's Tour in Glamorgan, 1775', *Glamorgan Historian* 1 (1963).
Cardiff Times, 12 March 1910.

See also: Cadw/ICOMOS; RCAHMW, *Inventory* Vol.IV; Lloyd; Newman.

Fonmon Castle, Penmark

Below:
Fonmon Castle south
façade, 1968.

Fonmon Castle, in Penmark, lies on the western lip of a steep ravine in which the Fonmon brook runs towards its confluence with the Kenson river. Medieval in origin, Fonmon Castle is believed to have been built by members of the St John family in the late twelfth to early thirteenth century. It remained in possession of the St Johns until the seventeenth century when it was purchased, as part of the Fonmon estate, by the parliamentarian Colonel Philip Jones whose descendants, the Boothby family, still live there.

From *c.*1200 until the mid-fourteenth century the St Johns were resident at Fonmon, their medieval castle forming three sides of an open court, a form which it retained until the seventeenth century. But in the 1430s Oliver St John married the heiress Margaret Beauchamp of Bletsoe in Bedfordshire and Fonmon became a secondary residence for the St Johns whose enhanced social position was soon to be reflected in their elevation to the peerage as Barons St John and Earls of Bolingbroke. A long period of absentee landlords and successive tenants came to an end soon after the sale of the Fonmon estate to Colonel Philip Jones in 1656. Having leased the castle to a tenant for a few years Jones finally took up residence there himself, in a property which was described in contemporary documents as 'much in decay' and 'no better than a farmhouse'. The colonel's programme of improvement extended not only to the castle itself but also to its gardens, and all subsequent developments of the gardens at Fonmon would be closely linked to major phases of rebuilding and improvement at the castle.

The walled, terraced and informal gardens which today surround the house on level ground on three sides probably have their origins in Colonel Philip Jones's late seventeenth-century improvements, foremost of which was the substantial enlargement of the castle. An estate map of the 1760s, the earliest evidence of the garden layout, shows a complicated, irregular pattern of walled enclosures around the house, a walled enclosure to the north (now the kitchen garden) and a number of walled enclosures south of the castle around the keep. Most of these elements appear to have been established before the major alterations to house and grounds carried out by Robert Jones III (1738-93) and can, with reasonable certainty, be attributed to Colonel Philip or his immediate successor. A large orchard is also shown on the 1760s map, on sloping ground to the north of the castle.

The second main phase of improvements at Fonmon was undertaken by Robert Jones III. The date 1762, engraved on a sundial on the exterior wall of the castle's south-east tower, commemorates the marriage of Robert and the heiress Jane Seys of Boverton and also marks the beginning of the transformation of the castle into an elegant eighteenth-century residence with a magnificent first floor long drawing room, impressive staircase hall and wealth of rococo ornamentation. A new pattern of fenestration, with deep sash windows, brought sunlight flooding into the principal south-facing rooms and afforded clear views into the gardens which were redesigned as part of the overall improvements.

Above: Detail from Fonmon estate map showing castle and gardens, 1830 (by kind permission of Sir Brooke Boothby).

Above:
Window overlooking
south lawn.

The tithe map of 1840 shows the extent of Robert Jones III's improvements to the gardens. All the walls to the south of the castle have been removed, with the exception of those surrounding the detached watch tower or keep shown on the 1760s map. This tall, battlemented tower which still stands in the south-east corner of the south lawn is something of an enigma. At one time interpreted as a medieval angle tower of a former outer court of the castle which had made way for later terraced gardens, it is now thought to have been erected (or rebuilt) as a pseudo-medieval folly by Robert Jones III, drawing its inspiration from the post-medieval watch tower at St Donats and incorporating re-used medieval dressed stone. From the long sash windows overlooking the lawn, the keep or watch tower would have been, as it still is, an eye-catching feature of the garden landscape. The north and west walls of the 'Keep Garden' survived until the late nineteenth century when they were removed by the then owner of Fonmon, Robert Oliver Jones, to open up the whole garden area even further. Today, a few specimen trees, including a cedar and a plane, stand on the south end of the lawn. And on the east edge of the lawn, above the ravine, are two specimen beech trees, one a superb copper beech heavily buttressed where its roots have caused the ravine's retaining wall to bulge significantly. Almost two hundred years old, these trees either survived the denuding of the estate of its mature timber (mainly elm) at the time of the Napoleonic wars or were planted in the immediate aftermath of that war.

The tithe map also depicts the stable block to the south-west of the castle, a range of buildings created by Robert Jones III from a late medieval barn. The long, straight ha-ha which runs south from the stable block is also believed to date from the late eighteenth century and to have been part of the wider scheme of defining the gardens, isolating them from the parkland to the west, and enhancing the aspect from the house.

Below: The Ravine, c.1965.

Above: Watchtower, 1999.

Today, many features of the historic garden landscape of Fonmon can still be identified. An early nineteenth-century engraving shows some ornamental planting on the slopes of the ravine below the castle, and while those slopes are now covered with invasive vegetation, including the dreaded Japanese knotweed, and any vestiges of ornamental planting have long since been overwhelmed, there still lie hidden in the undergrowth remains of the pools and cascades which were a Victorian feature of this area. Seven gardeners are known to have been employed here in the 1870s.

Below:
Lower Walled Garden
with glasshouses,
2006.

North of the house, the orchard shown on the 1760s map survives, within it a number of old apple trees, one of which has defied positive identification. The orchard no longer extends down the slope on the east of its site and the small conifer plantation within it is of recent planting.

Below: Large Walled Garden, 2006.

The series of walled gardens north of the house and adjacent to the orchard depicted on the 1760s map and in more detail on a map of the Fonmon estate prepared by the Cardiff surveyor G. Strawson in 1830 survive, in essential form, today. In the Lower Walled Garden are a number of brick-based greenhouses, one of which contains a mature vine bearing white Muscat grapes. An older vine in an adjacent greenhouse was removed by the present owner's father to accommodate his fine collection of orchids. From the Lower Walled Garden a gateway leads into the main kitchen garden (the Large Walled Garden), where the overall layout with large central beds, wide borders, central and perimeter paths, is largely a survival from the Victorian era. This garden is still highly productive of vegetables and flowers; its small herb garden, contained within clipped box hedges, is a

Below: Thatched summerhouse in Scented Garden, 2006.

Below:
Circular pond.

fairly recent creation. The third walled compartment is the Scented Garden where a thatched summerhouse has recently been erected. Beyond this is another walled enclosure, with random planting, from which a gateway in the east wall gives access to the lawn bordering the north side of the entrance drive. Across the lawn, alongside an entrance to the main kitchen garden, is a small circular ornamental pool fed from a well near the entrance gates to the castle. A border beneath the garden wall at the west end of the lawn contains a wide variety of fuschias. Clara, Lady Boothby, the present owner's grandmother, was founder president of the British Fuchsia Society, and many of the hardy

Fonmon Castle
fuchsia border, 2007.

Fonmon Castle gardens, 2007.

and other varieties of fuchsias planted by her in the garden survive to the present day. It was Clara, Lady Boothby who initiated the random planting in the Scented Garden, and her descendants have continued to embellish the gardens with new plantings of trees, shrubs and other decorative plants.

Of the changes made to the gardens and wider grounds of the castle by its owners in the nineteenth and twentieth centuries the most significant were the construction of the great retaining wall on the east side of the garden and the diversion of the driveway to its present course. Some time before 1878 the main drive, which had formerly run in a northerly direction to the front entrance on the south façade of the castle, was diverted to the west to arrive at the newly created main entrance on the west side of the house. Walls which had enclosed the keep garden on its north and west sides were removed; the south wall of the keep garden was extended westwards to the ha-ha but was subsequently removed. Evidence of this earlier pattern of walling can still be discerned beneath the south lawn.

One of the most recent improvements to the gardens has been the reinstatement of the small artificial waterfall and ornamental pond in the 'Dell', the deep hollow below the south lawn's retaining wall, the restoration of flights of stone steps leading down the slope and the planting of ferns which, it is assumed, were a Victorian feature of this part of the garden.

Hilary M. Thomas

Right: West front of house, 1999.

Gardens and castle open on Tuesday and Wednesday afternoons from April to September. At other times by appointment. Admission charges apply.

Sources

Primary
Survey of the estates of Robert Jones, *pre* 1767 (GRO D/DF vol. 26).
Penmark tithe award, 1840.
Map of the Fonmon Castle estate of Robert Jones Esq., by G. Strawson, 1830.
Information from Sir Brooke Boothby.

Secondary
Patricia Moore, *Fonmon Castle* (GRO, revised edition 1985).
Cardiff Times, 7 May 1910.

See also: Cadw/ICOMOS; RCAHMW *Inventory,* Vol.IV; Newman.

The Ham, Llantwit Major

The Ham, Llar

Top Right: Old Ham house, east front.

Bottom Right: The Wyatt mansion east front, photograph by Edwin Miles, early C20th (Glamorgan Record Office).

The area known as The Ham lies on the coastal edge of the Vale of Glamorgan, between Llantwit Major and Boverton. Of the house which stood on the site for centuries and was home to generations of the Nicholl family there is nothing left standing, and of the gardens which surrounded the house only faint traces remain. The 'original' sixteenth/seventeenth-century house of modest and singularly eccentric proportions was replaced in the 1860s by a grand Victorian Gothic mansion designed by Matthew Digby Wyatt. This massive house dominated the local landscape until it was gutted by fire after the Second World War and subsequently demolished in the 1960s. The loss of these houses is to be regretted, but a cause of equal if not greater regret is the loss of the magnificent gardens of The Ham, and in particular the Victorian terraces and balustrading which were such a feature of the grounds.

The Ham house stood on an area of level ground above steep slopes, the approach from the east side being particularly steep, and this configuration of the landscape determined in large measure the layout of the gardens. The formal walled gardens known to have existed close to the house in the eighteenth century had probably been created centuries earlier. The flight of thirty-six stone steps leading up the slope to the main east entrance of the house are said to have been brought to The Ham early in the eighteenth century, from the ruined Old Place in Llantwit Major, by the Reverend Iltyd Nicholl who is also credited with putting up ornamental iron gates at the foot of the steps and 'recycling' mullions from the windows at the Old Place to form pillars at either end of the steps.

Above: Terrace and balustrading, photograph by Edwin Miles, early C20th (Glamorgan Record Office).

The building of the new Wyatt mansion demanded that the grounds of The Ham be improved to match the grandeur of the house, and what was created here in the last quarter of the nineteenth century was a spectacular example of Victorian garden design on a grand scale, with formal lawns and terraces, neat flower beds and trimmed shrubberies complemented by informal 'wild' and 'bog' gardens, ponds and cascades. Among the many mature trees in the grounds remarked upon by visitors were ancient yews and chestnuts and a magnificent plane tree, but these along with others planted as part of the nineteenth-century (or earlier) scheme of design have not survived.

Right: Entrance front of the Wyatt mansion, photograph by Edwin Miles, early C20th (Glamorgan Record Office).

Above: Ornamental gates photograph by Edwin Miles, early C20th (Glamorgan Record Office).

It was on the east side of the house, where the ground fell and rose again so dramatically, that the greatest opportunity for garden design presented itself and was enthusiastically grasped by members of the Nicholl family. Work at The Ham coincided with the High Victorian revival of terraced gardens and many parallels can be made between the gardens at The Ham and those at Bowood in Wiltshire and Shrublands in Suffolk. A succession of terraces with magnificent ornamental stonework, for which the Elizabethan stonework at Haddon Hall in Derbyshire seems to have been the inspiration, was constructed, flanked by pillars and bisected by short flights of stone steps which replaced the long (and doubtless well-worn) staircase of earlier centuries. Ornamental gates, of delicately intricate design, were now placed at the top of the steps between stone pillars providing a 'clairevoie' across the valley. From this vantage point the eye was led across level ground and a croquet lawn at the foot of the terraces to a large oval pool with a central fountain. This was backed by a balustraded walkway with a single-arched alcove at one end and central three-arched loggia, the whole effect of which, with water feature, stone steps, niches, pergola and loggia was essentially Italianate.

Right: Lower terrace and croquet lawn, photograph by Edwin Miles, early C20th (Glamorgan Record Office).

*Above: Detail
of balustrading,
photograph by Edwin
Miles, early C20th
(Glamorgan Record
Office).*

*Right: Sundial,
photograph by Edwin
Miles, early C20th
(Glamorgan Record
Office).*

Above: Mr Symmonds, head gardener at The Ham, early C20th.

Photographs taken by the Bridgend photographer Edwin Miles in 1912 show the high quality of the stonework at The Ham, not just the walling and balustrading but also the decorative stone urns and pommels on the terraces and elsewhere in the garden, and a singularly engaging cherub sundial near the loggia. A local mason, Edward George, is revealed as the 'maker and builder' of all the stonework, a remarkable achievement still acknowledged on one of the surviving stone pillars of the former terracing where the initials EG are carved alongside those of the owner of The Ham, the man responsible for some of the garden design, Iltyd Nicholl.

Following the demolition of The Ham in the 1960s the whole site became part of a development for static 'park' homes which is what it remains today. The gardens, long overgrown and neglected, succumbed to the assaults of bulldozers and concrete mixers. Only the loggia with adjacent stone steps and walling, the vestiges of the pergola and the ornamental pool survived relatively unscathed and remain to the present day. Elsewhere on the site it is difficult to find traces of the once magnificent gardens, just the occasional short stretch of walling or balustrading among the uniform rows of park homes.

Right: The Ham in decline.

Right: View from loggia, photograph by Edwin Miles, early C20th (Glamorgan Record Office).

Below: View from loggia, 2002.

Above: South front of Castle, and gardens, 2004 (copyright: Vale of Glamorgan Council).

At the beginning of the twentieth century the privately owned Hensol Castle estate was extolled for 'its wonderfully Timbered Park, its famous Lakes and Ponds, and its attractive Gardens'. Its role as a hospital for most of the twentieth century inevitably brought changes, some occasioned by financial restrictions and manpower shortages, some by the need to create 'pleasure gardens' in the immediate vicinity of the new hospital buildings, but such changes have not materially affected the grand design of this important landscape park. Now, at the beginning of the twenty-first century, the future of Hensol Castle and the parkland are under review. It seems likely that they will become part of the adjoining hotel and spa development. The hope must be that any future development will be sympathetic to the historic nature of the site.

Derrick C. Kingham

In private ownership. Limited public access.

Sources

Primary
Hensol Castle sale catalogue, 1923 (GRO D/D Au).

See also: Cadw/ICOMOS; Malkin; Newman; Nicholas.

Llanblethian, village gardens

Today, Llanblethian is one of the most sought-after villages for those looking to make their home in the Vale of Glamorgan. Much the same applied two hundred years ago, and property advertisements in the *Cambrian* sang the praises of Llanblethian as not only being near to the fashionable market town of Cowbridge and to the coach route to London, but also containing houses suitable for 'gentlemen and officers on half pay'. Thomas Carlyle described the Llanblethian of around 1800 as 'a decidedly cheerful group of human homes, the greater part of them indeed belonging to persons of refined habits'. Many of the gardens of these houses reflected the prosperity of their owners or, perhaps, of their tenants.

Among the houses were Great House, Llanblethian House, Llanblethian Cottage, Hill House and The Cross, and outside the village Crossways, Marlborough and Breach. By 1850 The Verlands and St Quentin's could be added to the list. These were substantial houses, some of which have since disappeared and some whose gardens have been much altered. Nevertheless, enough remains in Llanblethian today to give an echo of some of Llanblethian's gardens of the past.

Above: Llanblethian Cottage, watercolour by W.H. Taynton, c.1850 (by kind permission of John Edmondes).

Llanblethian Cottage was where Edward and John Sterling lived between 1809 and 1814. Writing later, John Sterling described it thus:

> 'my home was built upon the slope of a hill, with a little orchard stretching down before it, and a garden rising behind … The narrow orchard, with its grove of old apple trees; the garden where I sowed flower-seeds, and then turned up the ground again and planted potatoes, and then rooted out the potatoes to insert acorns and apple pips, and at last, as may be supposed, reaped neither roses, nor potatoes, nor oak-apples, nor apples …'.

Like many houses in Llanblethian, this property was tenanted by a succession of relatively wealthy families. After the Sterlings came Charles Courtenay, one of the Warwickshire Throckmortons who, in the next four years, carefully planted fruit trees (pears – 'winter Beure, swan egg and a Chaumontelle'. greengages, double Gloucester cherries, a Moor Park apricot and a vine), ornamental trees and shrubs (laburnums, spiraeas, Portugal laurels, Persian lilacs, phillyrea, guelder roses and hypericum), and vegetables. Unusually, we have the names of the gardener, William Davy, who was paid 2s.0d. a day, his specialist helper Thomas Thomas who pruned the vine for 3s.6d. a day, and the occasional assistant Thomas Jones.

*Below: Hill House,
late C20th.*

Watercolour sketches made in the latter half of the nineteenth century, including that by W.H. Taynton *c.*1850, clearly show the enclosing walls of the gardens running steeply up Llanblethian Hill behind the house. Even though Llanblethian Cottage was demolished *c.*1900 to make way for the Vicarage (now The Old Vicarage), those walls remain, creating a terraced effect on the hillside.

Adjoining this property was **Hill House,** which today has attractive and varied gardens, the layout of which seems in part to date back well over a hundred years. Another steep site, it was terraced and subdivided into

smaller enclosures for decorative purposes, kitchen gardens and orchards. The house was owned by the Reverend Jonathan Morgan from 1795, and on his death ownership passed to his wife and then to his niece Ann Thomas, and it is possible that the Morgans and Ann Thomas were responsible for the original layout of the gardens. William Thomas, maltster and manure dealer, was there from at least 1871 to 1892 and he and his family must certainly have helped to maintain the property. The rock garden and pergola, pleasant features of the property today, were designed by Alan Gibbs who lived in the house in the 1940s.

Further up the hill towards the church is **The Cross,** essentially a substantial Victorian villa, with a delightful garden consisting largely of lawns and

Above: The Cross, photograph by Edwin Miles, early C20th (Glamorgan Record Office).

shrubberies. Probably laid out between 1852 and 1870 when the owner was Margaret Entwisle, member of a wealthy Lancashire family (who had lived for a short time at Llanblethian Cottage and then at Crossways), it was maintained and extended by F.W. Dunn who was the owner when Edwin Miles took a series of photographs of the gardens (photographs deemed worthy of being sold as postcards!). Today there are some fine well-established trees: a Wellingtonia *(Sequoiadendron giganticum)* near the gates, and pines and yews running along the northern boundary of the property on the steep slopes of Llanblethian hill.

On the other side of the valley, towards the castle, stands **St Quentin's House,** a pleasing late-Georgian property whose garden is first mentioned in a conveyance of 1824. In 1918, W.F. Evans, the headmaster of Cowbridge Grammar School, retired to St Quentin's and brought Harry Evans with him from the school as gardener. 'W.F.' thought sufficiently well of Harry to leave him a bequest in his will. A number of subsequent owners have put their mark on the gardens: Stanley Philpot, an architect and surveyor from Tunbridge Wells, between 1928 and 1939, Blanche Homfray from 1940 to 1947, the Walters brothers from 1947 to 1952, and Sir David Llewellyn MP and his wife Joan to 1962.

Below: Sketch of St Quentin's House, 1831 (by kind permission of John Edmondes).

In 1911 the castle was occupied by the Ebsworth family and an account of the gardens at that time reveals that a Wild Garden, a Sundial Garden and a Rose Garden enhanced the natural surroundings of the house. Also mentioned were glasshouses against south facing walls in which peaches, nectarines and vines were grown and where delicate ornamental shrubs were propagated. Photographs of the period underline the varied content of the gardens and one recently discovered photograph shows the 'Dutch Garden' (probably also known as the Sundial Garden) simply laid out with lawn, central path with sundial, and an open fronted garden room in a walled enclosure below the castle to the south-west of the parish church.

When Sir Sidney Byass bought Llandough Castle in 1914 and the Byass family moved into the house the gardens were still in their heyday. They remained so for some years after the death of Sir Sidney in 1929 and the subsequent departure of his wife from Llandough, tended by William Harkness's immediate successor Richard German who, in turn, was followed by Jack Evans. In the 1930s the castle was leased by Lady Byass to the Ministry of Labour and was used as a Juvenile Instruction Centre for boys whose health had suffered as a result of working in the mines. Many years after the closure of the centre in 1939 the former superintendent recalled the ample quantities of vegetables, flowers and fruit (including figs, nectarines and peaches) grown in the castle gardens and the prize chrysanthemums grown by head gardener Jack Evans. Photographs of the boys exercising and relaxing against a backdrop of well tended lawns and flower borders close to the house also record the creation of a swimming pool out of an existing lily pond.

Below Left: Creation of swimming pool, c.1938 (Glamorgan Record Office).

Right: The swimming pool, 1984.

Above: The glasshouses, 1930s (Glamorgan Record Office).

After the War the whole content and appearance of the castle and its gardens were drastically changed. The central section of the house was demolished, the main surviving portion now formed the main 'Llandough Castle' residence, the former servants' quarters to the east were converted into flats. Parts of the gardens (including the former kitchen garden) reverted to nature, parts were separated from the castle when outbuildings were converted into residences and land was sold for house building. Within the perimeter wall of the castle itself a new swimming pool was built in the lawned area immediately west of the house. The former orchard to the south-west of the church, and the old gardeners' bothy all disappeared in the 1960s when houses were built in 'Castle Precinct'.

A few stone walls, a few old trees, a few woodland walks and remnants of water features in the woods are but faint reminders of once impressive gardens. The gardens of Llandough Castle are yet another addition to the long list of Glamorgan's 'lost gardens'.

Hilary M. Thomas

Above: Yew tree in Castle grounds.

Private residence. No public right of access.

Sources

Primary
Giles family photograph album (in GRO).
Juvenile Instruction Centre notes and photographs, 1936-9 (GRO D/DX 865).

Secondary
Hilary M. Thomas, 'Llandough Castle, near Cowbridge', *Morgannwg*, XXXIII (1989).
Cardiff Times, 16 December 1911.
Roger Lee Brown (ed.), *The Letters of Edward Copleston, Bishop of Llandaff, 1828-1849* (Cardiff, South Wales Record Society, 2003).

See also: Newman; Royal Commission, *The Later Castles*.

Llanmihangel Place,

Llanmihang

Far Right: Detail from estate map showing house and gardens, 1770s (Glamorgan Record Office).

Llanmihangel is one of those rare places in the Vale of Glamorgan where the imprint of the past has defied the passage of centuries. The imposing Tudor mansion, Llanmihangel house (alias Plas Llanmihangel), described 'as one of the finest and most complete examples of an early Tudor gentry house in Glamorgan', stands near the bottom of a south-facing slope above the little valley of the Nant Llanmihangel, in an unspoilt rural enclave. House, contemporary farm buildings and medieval church together form an integrated and harmonious historic landscape where time seems to have stood still.

Dominating that landscape is the Tudor mansion, believed to have been built by James Thomas, sheriff of Glamorgan in 1551. It contains within its core fabric of an earlier house which existed on the site when the first members of the Thomas family acquired Llanmihangel, but by the middle of the sixteenth century the Thomases were sufficiently wealthy and influential to transform their property into a model of Tudor fashion. When, in the wake of the Civil War, good fortune deserted the Thomas family a wealthy London merchant, Humphrey Edwin, acquired Llanmihangel, and from the Edwins the property descended to the Wyndham family and ultimately to the earls of Dunraven. The house that James Thomas built for his large family in the sixteenth century has survived virtually intact into the twenty-first century, little changed by minor improvements carried out by successive owners and occupiers. It is a remarkable survival.

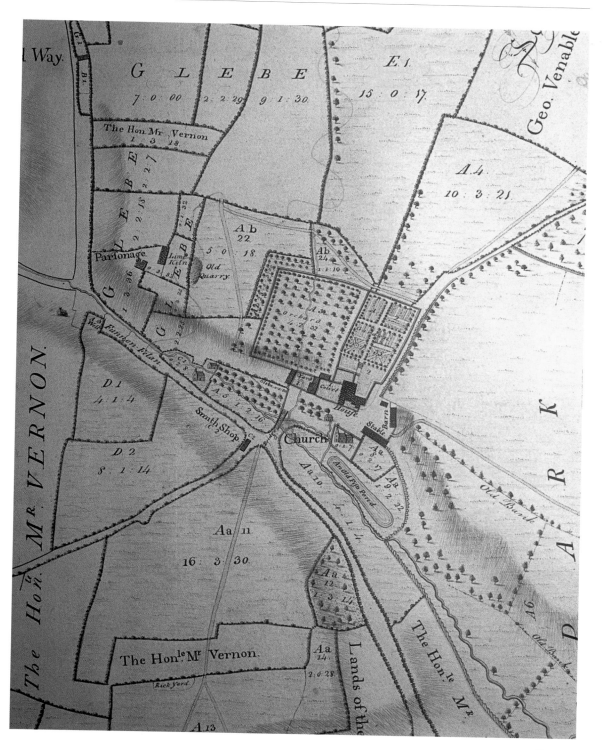

Way.

GLEBE

7 . 0 . 00   2 . 2 . 29   9 . 1 . 30

E . 1

15 : 0 : 17

Geo. Venable

The Hon Mr Vernon
1 . 3 . 18

A . 4

10 : 3 : 21

G L E B E
2 . 2 . 7

G L E B E
2 . 2 . 18

Ab
22

5 . 0 . 18

Ab
24

Parsonage

Lime Kiln

Old Quarry

G L E B E

Orchard

Mr VERNON.

D . 1
4 . 1 . 4

Smith Shop

Church

House

Stable Barn

Aa
7

D . 2
8 . 1 . 14

Aa 10

Aa 11

16 : 3 : 30

Old Park Pond

R

K

Aa
12

Old Bridle

The Hon^le Mr Vernon.

Rick Yard

Aa
14
2 . 0 . 28

Lands of the

The Hon^le M^r

The Hon^u Mr VERNON.

A . 13

Even more remarkable are the gardens which survive at Llanmihangel. Such a prestigious property demanded attractive pleasure gardens where, in the sixteenth and seventeenth centuries, formality and privacy could be combined and from which the surrounding countryside could be excluded. Like the house itself, the gardens have survived from the date of their creation, their survival due in large measure to centuries of neglect during which few attempts were made to improve them in conformity with current fashion. Eventually their maintenance lapsed and nature was allowed to take over. Today, the impact of time and nature has altered almost beyond recognition the neat, clipped formality of the original design, but the main features of that design and its underlying symmetry can still be discerned.

Right: Llanmihangel, watercolour by Charlotte Louisa Traherne, c.1830 (by kind permission of the McLaggan family).

The estate map of the 1770s shows the layout of the gardens at that date. The main area of garden lies on the south-facing slope behind the house, and what is depicted here is a seventeenth-century formal garden with grass terraces linked by two flights of stone steps, a broad central avenue running north to south through the third terrace with axial paths bordering formal beds with geometric patterns. Beds and paths are lined with clipped trees and shrubs. Beyond this pleasure garden, to the west, lies the orchard, neatly laid out with rows of fruit trees and bisected by a stream, and beyond this a shelter belt to give protection from the prevailing wind. The entire garden area is confined within stone walls with a pillared gateway giving access to the pleasure garden from the north end of the central avenue. In 1629 there was published John Parkinson's treatise on garden design *Paradisi in Sole, Paradisus Terrestris. A Garden of Pleasant Flowers* which contains a plan of a formal garden layout, the essential elements of which are a pleasure garden with geometric beds and paths, an orchard and a shelter belt of trees. It is a layout instantly recognisable at Llanmihangel where the entire main garden occupies an area of approximately 8 acres (3.2ha) and the pleasure garden about a third of that acreage.

It is probable that the garden was first laid out by members of the Thomas family and that the stone walls enclosing the gardens, at least some of the terracing and probably the lower flight of terrace steps can be attributed to the Thomases in the later sixteenth century. The sophisticated pattern of yew-lined walks within that framework, as depicted on the 1770s map, is generally agreed to have been the work of Sir Humphrey Edwin who acquired Llanmihangel in 1685. Edwin, whose life and activities until then had centred on London, would have been familiar with the capital's gardens where Dutch and Continental influences were strong and where the fashion was for 'green' gardens. That fashion was reinforced with the accession of William III who praised evergreens as the greatest addition to the beauty of a garden (Edwin, as sheriff of London & Middlesex, welcomed William and Mary to the capital in 1688) and when Edwin took possession of Llanmihangel it can be assumed that he made his garden there a model of green fashion.

Below: Central yew avenue, 2006.

Above: Terrace steps, 2001.

Until the late nineteenth century the yews and other evergreens which would have included holly, box (which may have edged the formal beds), bay and laurel were kept neatly clipped. In his *Topographical Dictionary* published in 1833 Samuel Lewis wrote of Llanmihangel's collection of evergreens as 'the finest to be met with in this part of the principality … renowned for the luxuriance of their growth … [and] perhaps unrivalled by any in the country'. By the end of that century luxuriance had been allowed to run wild and the garden had taken on an altogether untamed appearance, although some of the then massive yews forming the central and side avenues did still show evidence 'of having once been bushes before they were allowed freedom to run into trees'.

That freedom is even more apparent today when towering yews (survivors or successors of those planted by Edwin) dominate the garden, where stumps and decaying timber are evidence of yews which have succumbed to age and

Above: Perimeter walk, 2001.

the elements, and where the old pattern of avenue and paths has been largely obscured. But the two flights of stone steps survive and beneath the grassy paths stone setts are still in place. A few, a very few, hollies and laurels can still be found, and the boundary walls (much restored) still stand. Within the orchard are a few ancient apple and pear trees, and a couple of walnut trees, but no survivors of the filberts, and the fig tree 'as old as the time of the Edwins' remarked upon by the antiquarian David Jones of Wallington in the 1880s. The same observer refers to the former deer park to the east of the house, the low boundary wall of which was once topped by high palings, and he also mentions the old west boundary wall of the 'pleasaunce' (gardens) which had been taken down during alterations and improvements carried out by the Dunraven estate agent John Franklen who was resident in

Above: Both flights of terrace steps, 2001.

the house from the 1750s until his death in 1824. According to David Jones, Elizabethan ladies had shot deer with bow and arrow through diagonal slits in the stonework of this west wall, but as there is no evidence of the existence of a deer park at Llanmihangel in the Elizabethan period, this statement remains suspect.

The walled courtyard at the front of the house as depicted on the 1770s map, an enclosure which probably contained a small formal garden from the time of the Thomases onwards, was replaced in the nineteenth century by a terraced garden which survives to the present day.

House and garden inevitably over the centuries attracted their own legends, attractive myths perpetuated by some uncritical antiquarians. The house had its ghost. The gardens were said to have royal and biblical associations. But Queen Anne's visit to Llanmihangel and the planting of a yew tree to commemorate the visit has no place in history and with whom, one wonders, originated the tale of a yew tree being planted at Llanmihangel for every day of the year, only the one planted on Good Friday failing to grow?

The history of the Thomases of Llanmihangel reaches out from the confines of the Vale of Glamorgan into the world of national political events, as does that of the Edwins and their successors. The Thomas family played a prominent and for them financially disastrous role in the Civil War. Humphrey Edwin's 'career' in the official life of London was crowned in 1697 by his appointment as lord mayor. The last generation of the Thomases to live at Llanmihangel was too impoverished to contemplate improvement of the property. The Edwins spent as much, if not more, of their time in London as in Llanmihangel and

while they did make some alterations to the house the main impact of their period of ownership is seen in the gardens (and in the grandiose monuments in Llanmihangel church where they lie buried). When Charles Wyndham succeeded to the estate in 1777 he contemplated building a new house at Llanmihangel, but fortunately he transferred his ambitions to his property at Dunraven where his successor Thomas Wyndham erected a Gothic castle, and Llanmihangel house and gardens were spared.

At first sight, the sloping pasture land south and east of the ruined mansion now shows little sign of the superb gardens known to have complemented the house in its heyday. G.T. Clark's description of the site in 1867 suggests that some features of the gardens were then still visible – 'the position of the house, on ground sloping towards the south was favourable for the construction of terraced gardens, and full advantage seems to have been taken of this. The ground to the north, falling towards the house, is retained by a wall and terrace towards the west. West again, of the house … the middle platform is retained by another wall …'. Since Clark's day nature has encroached to a much greater extent upon the site of the gardens, masking but not destroying features glimpsed by Clark and his contemporaries. Recent expert examination of the land immediately adjacent to the ruins of the old house has revealed that the structure of those gardens has survived intact, and that hidden in the landscape are many significant features of a formally laid-out garden with terraces, walled compartments, walks and ponds. These represent a remarkable survival from the sixteenth and early seventeenth centuries, a survival due in no small part to neglect and comparable in that respect with Llanmihangel.

The house itself stood on a platform above two walled terraces descending down the gentle slope from the churchyard towards the Nant Llantrithyd in the valley bottom where rectilinear fishponds were linked by the canalised, stone-lined stream. From the north-east corner of the house a raised walkway led down into the gardens over a bridge (now collapsed, but of which evidence survives) and up again by wide stone steps to a look-out platform or gazebo on the far side of the valley. The raised walkway 'an advanced feature for a provincial garden' invites comparisons with the cloister walk at the Carmarthenshire mansion, Aberglasney, and the fact that the Rudds of Aberglasney and the Aubreys of Llantrithyd were connected by marriage may be significant in this context. As far as can be ascertained, the creation of the gardens was begun by John Basset and continued by his Mansel and Aubrey successors. Rice Merrick in his *Book of Glamorganshires Antiquities*, written in 1578, credited Anthony Mansel with the creation of the fishponds, and it is Anthony Mansel who is believed to have created the impressive walled and terraced gardens which led down to the fishponds.

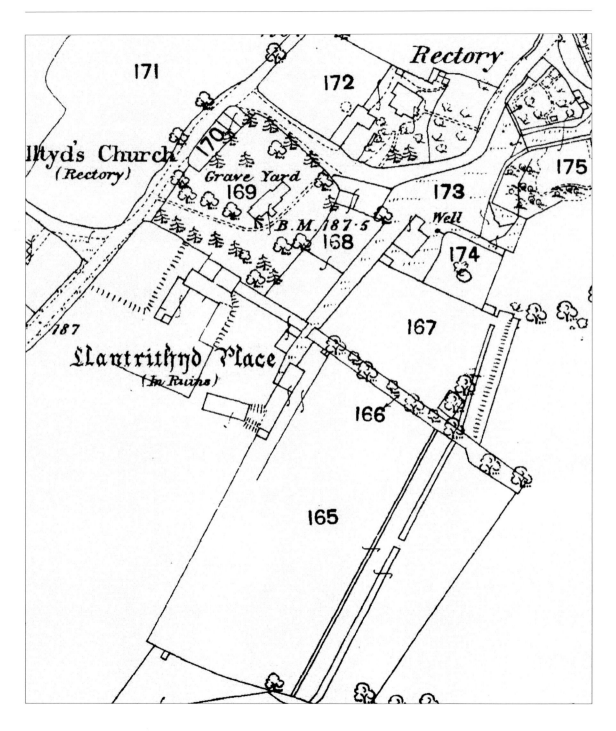

Above: Detail from First Edition Ordnance Survey map, 1878.

Above: Aerial view of Llantrithyd Place, 2001 (copyright: Geo Information Group).

Above: Raised walk in the ruined gardens of Llantrithyd (Cadw: Crown Copyright / E. Whittle).

Below: Block plan of grounds (RCAHMW. Crown Copyright).

In 1652 the Water Poet, John Taylor, described Llantrithyd as 'a Welsh Paradise for building, situation, pleasure and plenty'; the household accounts of Sir Thomas Aubrey of Llantrithyd in the late sixteenth and early seventeenth centuries provide insights into the enviable wealth and status of the Aubrey family. Included in the accounts are references to the gardens – the 'leading' of the summerhouse in the upper garden in 1635, the purchase of statues for the gardens in 1627, and the buying of nectarine and cherry trees for the orchard in the 1620s and 1630s. The overall impression given by these and other references is that Sir Thomas's gardens were fashionable, impressive in design and content, and well maintained. The sophistication of the garden layout must have significantly enhanced the architectural grandeur of the mansion house itself, and it is interesting to note that the gardens at Old Beaupre, St Hilary, created by Bassets and Mansels in the sixteenth and seventeenth centuries, were also models of contemporary garden fashion with terraced walks leading down to the river and ornamental ponds.

Beyond the Llantrithyd gardens to the north and east, and separated from them not only by walls and fences but also by the parish road, there survives remarkably intact a large deer park of some 80 acres which was almost certainly created by Sir John Aubrey sometime after 1660. The park, of which no mention is made in a survey of the Aubrey manors of 1643, appears on John Ogilby's map of 1675 as 'Sir John Aubry Park' and was stocked with fallow deer. Disparked c.1900 the park was restocked with red and fallow deer in 1990. The perimeter

Left: The ruined mansion, 2000.

walls and internal paddocks surviving from the seventeenth century have provide the essential structures for deer farming in the twentieth and twenty-first centuries.

Sir Thomas Aubrey's household accounts, as indicated above, provide glimpses into the gardens at Llantrithyd in the seventeenth century, but not until the 1780s is there again clear documentary reference to the gardens. A survey by John Stone in 1788 describes two kitchen gardens of approximately one acre, two other gardens with a large greenhouse heated by stoves, walled gardens with their walls well-covered with [fruit] trees and a walled orchard containing 'choice fruit trees'. By the date of this survey the Aubreys had already begun to distance themselves from Llantrithyd and the gardens must soon have begun to deteriorate, although many of the essential features of the garden landscape were recorded a century later on the Ordnance Survey map of 1878. Not recorded on map or survey are the four bee boles which survive in a stone wall below the churchyard and within the area of the former upper terrace. Circumstantial evidence suggests a sixteenth- or seventeenth-century date for these structures. The sombre ruins of the house did attract occasional nineteenth-century photographers and amateur artists but, sadly, no maps or artists' impressions of the gardens in their heyday are known to exist. Left untended, to be reclaimed by nature, the gardens which had escaped the hands of eighteenth-century improvers and the fashion for 'informal' landscaping also escaped the imposition of later garden fashions. They are indeed a remarkable survival, but they do not reveal themselves to the casual eye, their documentation is scant, and their interpretation demands intensive, specialist investigation of the landscape.

Hilary M. Thomas

Site in private ownership. No public right of access.

Sources

Primary
Llantrithyd estate survey, 1788 (GRO D/DAu 32).

Secondary
Lloyd Bowen (ed.), *Family and Society in Early Stuart Glamorgan: The Household accounts of Sir Thomas Aubrey of Llantrithyd,* c.1565-1641 (South Wales Record Society, 2006).
G.T. Clark & R.O. Jones, 'Contributions towards a history of the parish of Llantrithyd', *Archaeologia Cambrensis,* 3rd series 12 (1866) and 13 (1867).
Brian Ll. James, 'The Parish of Llantrithyd', in *The Garden of Wales,* ed. Stewart Williams (Cowbridge, 1961).

See also: Cadw/ICOMOS; Carlisle; Merrick; Newman, *The Greater Houses.*

Merthyr Mawr House,
Merthyr Mawr

Sir John Nicholl's Creation

'It will be in future years that we shall thoroughly appreciate the value of records such as these. Not only will they be of the greatest use in establishing dates and in furnishing a history … of the various phases through which our neighbourhood has passed in its onward progress, but how delightful it will be in our old age to peruse in the early pages of 'Tiddle-Taddle' the records of our former struggles, successes and failures …'- thus wrote the editor of the Merthyr Mawr house magazine in 1859 soliciting pieces describing changes and improvements to gardens and grounds. He had earlier noted some horticultural events – the flowering in the hot house of an epiphytic orchid *(Dendrobium Nobile)* 'a credit to the Rev. Ed. Nicholl and Mr. Thos. Williams' and 'a fine specimen of Gynerium Argenteum *[Cortaderia Elegans*, pampas grass] with 27 heads'. But for the most part his readership was sadly deaf to his plea, and the garden history of Merthyr Mawr has to be inferred from records (labour journals, accounts, letters and diaries) made for other purposes, from sporadic plans, drawings and photographs, and from the gardens themselves.

Merthyr Mawr was and is the creation of Sir John Nicholl, who to the writer would be more completely a hero if he had not been too obviously one to himself. He was a second son in a Vale family of small squires and parsons. Born in 1759, he went to London and made a successful career in the law (and later as a member of parliament, a privy counsellor and a judge); he was knighted in 1798 upon his appointment as King's Advocate. In 1804, after protracted negotiations, he bought the run-down Merthyr Mawr estate, then of 800 acres or so, from the successors of Charles Bowen, to whom it had descended after the Stradlings of St Donats died out in 1738; it had been a small part of their extensive holdings for over three centuries. Sir John's purposes were to impress himself upon the land of his forebears (the family was conveniently too respectable to be an embarrassment, while not so eminent as to be impossible to outshine); to found a dynasty of his own; and to create a monument appropriate in scale and style to the dignity of the law and his profession of it. He succeeded in all three. More than a minnow in London, in Bridgend he would and did become a big fish. In case he should need reminding of the scope of his responsibilities, he was in the habit of enumerating the institutions and organisations in which he was active on the endpapers of his annual diary, from Privy Council to Horticultural Society. For 1820, of the thirty-two listed five were in Bridgend,

Below:
Portrait of Sir John Nicholl.

covering a wide field of local life – School, Savings Bank, District Committee for Christian Knowledge, Agricultural Society and Clergy Charity. As to his dynastic purpose, the seventh generation is now at Merthyr Mawr House. His monument is, of course, that house and its demesne. The creation of the house is a tale which has been told by Hilary M. Thomas; that of the garden, pleasure grounds and park is attempted here.

Sir John took a large and personal part in the designing and indeed the building of the house, and for its surrounds seems to have been effectively his own designer. It cannot have been easy for a man whose profession lay three days' travel away in London, even one whose favourite reading was 'Employment of Time' and whose self-imposed twenty-four hour regimen was '3 [hours] Dressing and Exercise, 2 Meals, 3 Family and Society, 8 Studies and Official Duties and 8 Sleep'. His library shows that he equipped himself both for dealing with practical issues and for ensuring familiarity with modern trends and fashions. On the shelves, well thumbed and bearing his bookplate are, among others, Speechly on the Vine, Forsyth on Fruit Trees, Weston on Practical Agriculture and Gardening, Marshall on Planting and Rural Ornament, Whately's, Gilpin's and Repton's respective Observations, and Payne Knight on Taste. In the

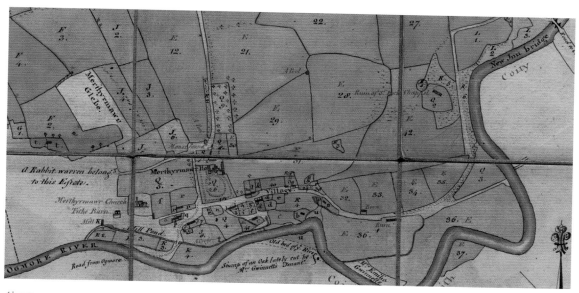

Above:
Detail from map of the
Merthyr Mawr estate,
by John Williams,
1794.

1820s he acquired Phillips's *Sylva Florifera* and Monteath's *Forester's Guide,* and reminded himself to buy Loudon's Encyclopaedia. He had subscribed to *Curtis's Botanical Magazine* from its start.

In 1806 work started on the new house and the demesne followed hard upon it. The change can be seen by comparing the 1794 survey by John Williams of the Bowen estate with a plan prepared by the polymath (or at least jack of all trades) William Weston Young in 1812, when he was commissioned to produce an imposing volume majestically entitled 'Maps of Estates the Property of the Right Honourable Sir John Nicholl, Knight, Dean of the Arches and Judge of the Prerogative Court of Canterbury'.

Young's map of the demesne shows what was formerly a block of seventeen fields and parts of fields, totalling over 142 acres, now girdled round (on its vulnerable frontiers) with substantial walls, and the area thus emparked completely recast into six lawns or meadows, with enclosures for pleasure grounds, and for woodland planting for amenity and shelter. The old Stradling manor house was pulled down for its stone and other materials, its walled gardens and orchard being left to supplement the produce to come from the three-quarter acre brick-lined kitchen garden which was constructed behind the stable block on the new site. (A new garden has recently been constructed within the site of the Stradling gardens – but that is another story!)

The site for the new house was carefully chosen to take advantage of local features; it was, after all, much cheaper to bring a house to a landscape than to create a landscape around a house. Scenes partaking (if in a modest degree) of the Romantic, the Picturesque, even of the Awful and the Sublime,

MAP of MERTHYR MAWR PLACE and DEMESNE
IN THE PARISH of MERTHYR MAWR IN THE COUNTY of GLAMORGAN

were available to be enjoyed at no cost. From the drawing room verandah there could be vistas westward to the ruins of Ogmore Castle and towards Candleston Castle and the golden flank of the highest sandhill in Britain; to the east, Coity Castle provided another borrowed eyecatcher, while nearer at hand were objectives for short and pleasant strolls – to the village with its

Below:
St Roque chapel,
C19th.

pleasing rusticity, to the sinuosities, cliffs and tumbled rocks of the Ogmore river, to the overhanging precipice of the Big Dell and the subsidiary holes and caverns formed by an underground stream (which might not quite be Alph the sacred river, but was undeniably Curious). Atop the rising ground behind the house was the little ruined chapel of St Roque, which presented an almost unbearably Romantic aspect after its embellishment by two large Celtic stones moved there by Sir John (and six oxen) after receiving a letter from Edward Williams (Iolo Morganwg) complaining that in their original positions they were being 'most shamefully mutilated by persons who break off parts … for whetting their scythes'.

These features fell easily into place around the new house. A major (and expensive) problem however, was the road to the village which followed the line of the present drive from near the New Inn Bridge before swinging

left-handed to join its present course south-east of the new site. To the south it could be discreetly concealed, and an uninterrupted view preserved by manipulation of the contours, but to the east it allowed the populace far too close for comfort. Various schemes of orientation of the buildings to minimize the impact of this vulgar intrusion were considered, but none was satisfactory, and estimates were obtained for the construction of three hundred yards of new road. The difficulty was that the new line included a river crossing. There seems to have been an existing track over a ford, but the Ogmore is a sizeable and flood-prone river, and for the only access to a village a new bridge was clearly necessary and Sir John had no option but to provide it. He commissioned his architect, Henry Wood, to produce designs - an expensive version with stone arches and a cheaper one with wooden superstructure. Sir John opted for the cheaper alternative and it was built in 1808. Unfortunately, by 1827 it had fallen into disrepair and Sir John's attempt to argue that it was now the responsibility of the public failed because he had – an uncharacteristic oversight – omitted to have it approved by the county surveyor, as required by statute. The stone bridge which he was forced to rebuild bears the face-saving inscription 'This bridge was dedicated and built at the expence of the Rt. Honourable Sir John Nicholl Kt. …'- as true, perhaps, as all monumental inscriptions should be, but also as misleading as many are. It is a final small irony that, after 180 years, the local name of the structure is still 'The Wooden Bridge'.

The main work of laying out and planting the park and pleasure grounds took place in 1808 and 1809. Sir John noted that 25,003 plants of 42 species in the nursery were to be transplanted in 1808, and he made planting plans for 49 species of trees and shrubs and grid patterns for 'mixing 100 trees' with versions for either 25 per cent or 50 per cent conifers presumably as a nurse. His list of shrubs included 'Laburnum, Sumach, Dogwood, Spanish Broom, Lilac, Guelderose, Laurel, Laurustinus, Phylerea, Siringa, Juniper, Savin, Arbor Vitae, Cedar, Althea Frutex, Spirea Frutex, Tutsan, Cistus, Rose, Honeysuckles, Jessamine, Bladder Senna, Redthorn, Sea Buckthorn, Ailanthus'. In 1809 he ordered from Lee and Kennedy 8500 trees 'from 3 to 5 feet' and 115 orchard trees, the majority being peach, nectarine, apricot, plum, apple and pear 'in sorts', but including cherries, quinces, figs, damsons and bullaces. Also from Lee and Kennedy came 'by the cart' 28 species of climbers (for example 'Clematis Cirrhosa, Viticella Caerulea, Viticella Rubra and Viticella plena, orientalis, virginiana and flammula') and more than 50 species of shrubs, mostly in fives. The great majority of the trees purchased

announcement in 1857 that recently 'many shrubs have been taken away, thus extending the view and giving a freer aspect to the place'.

Minnie's drawing also shows that the fence separating the garden from the park which appears prominently in a sketch by Young (presumably contemporaneous with his plans) has been replaced by a ha-ha. It is not clear precisely when this was done.

There are several mentions of sunk fences earlier than 1812. In January 1804 Sir John's diary records 'agreed with Matthew to dig the sunk round the plantation and Pleasure Ground to the west of the House 4 Feet deep, 7 Feet wide at top, 1 Foot wide at bottom and to wheel the earth so as to form the Ground on the West Front – 75 Yards at 6d. per cubic yard, digging and wheeling, but if the job turns out hard to give him 7d.'. He also made a sketch of a semi-sunk fence – a ditch faced with a masonry wall topped by a hedge of quicks planted to lean forward. There is also a reference in 1847 – '101 perches wall sunk fence South Lawn at 1/6d.' followed by a further fifteen perches. In 1858 the 'Tiddle-Taddle' reports that 'The new ha-ha and terrace at Merthyr Mawr have been again taken in hand and are making rapid progress.' At any rate it seems clear from the Ordnance Survey that by 1876 the ha-ha was complete in its present form. A quarter-mile long on the south side with a further 100 yards on the west and faced with a masonry wall over six feet high, it is very much a feature of the garden, even if it contravenes Repton's injunction that ha-has should be short, the easy leap which they afford to the eye being outweighed by the inconvenience to the body. Since in the last few years it has caused fractures to the knee, arm and pelvis of involuntary leapers, as well as destroying a new and expensive machine, Repton's advice may be considered prudent.

Below: Sketch by William Weston Young showing ha-ha.

Other changes between 1812 and 1876 are the extension westward of the wood behind the house, and the appearance of terracing in front of it. The former may have been dictated by experience of the destructive salt-laden westerly wind (which also required the sacrifice of Sir John's cherished vistas – though the growth of his own plantings had in any event made them hard to maintain). The quotation from the 'Tiddle-Taddle' above suggests that the terracing was done in the 1850s, and again may have been partly influenced by the requirements of the mowing machine which would not have appreciated the awkward slope down to the South Lawn. The logical further work of walling the banks between the terraces was not carried out for another half century, either as being a step too far in the direction of formality or (more likely) because it could not be afforded. Another development of the 1850s was the creation by John Cole Nicholl (and the mower) of a ground for cricket and archery – and later for the Glamorgan Lawn Tennis and Croquet Club – in the field south of the village road. The access was through the 'sally port', a vaulted tunnel created by Sir John as a private link to the river meadows. The development included a pavilion with 'bandstand', said to have been financed by John Cole's sale of his First Folio edition of Shakespeare.

Above: West lawn, late C20th.

Minnie was certainly fond of her garden, and her intermittent diaries particularly show her pride in the terrace flower beds. But life turned increasingly against her. In 1881 she wrote that she 'looked at the garden lists and found my wishes far too expensive!'. In the evening she looked again and 'tried to reduce expenditure!'. There was at that time one splurge in which a considerable number of shrubs and trees were bought and planted, some of which are identifiable today. They included a number of then recent introductions; mercifully the alkaline soil overlying limestone forbade most of the grosser Himalayan exotics! But that splurge was an exception. Minnie was in any event too free a spirit to be hemmed in by house and garden. Her taste was for the wild – for mountains and for climbing, for travel and nature, and when her husband died in 1894 she fell, forward rather than back, on these interests, leaving the tameness of gardening for her old age.

Merthyr Mawr was taken on by her eldest son, yet another John ('J.I.D.'), who had had the good sense to marry into a banking family. His wife was Eleanor Harford, and during their tenure the gardens reached their highest degree of formality and their greatest extent. The number of gardeners, which in 1875 had normally been three (unchanged from forty years earlier – and paid little more) was doubled. The fashion deities were now Jekyll and Lutyens, balanced by a tincture of Robinson, and following these influences much was done. Retaining walls were built for the terraces, with borders at their bases and bisected by stone steps, apparently in 1911. The middle terrace became a bowling green, with elaborate foundations and drainage. Immediately to the east of the lower terrace a small rockery was much enlarged, with a further extension to a tank garden. Long cutting borders appeared to the south of the walled garden, backed by fruit trees espaliered on to stout trellis. Immaculate gravel paths, immaculately edged, were everywhere, and J.I.D. is said to have sat in the verandah checking on the straightness of the lines made by the Dennis mower on the lawn.

There were two further large projects. Between the road and the river opposite the end of the back drive, two or three acres were laid out and planted as a bamboo garden. Photographs show it as a pretty place with little oriental bridges over the channelled streams, but it bore its own death warrant. The story goes that Hilliers' nursery, gratified by the size of the order, threw in some plants of *Sasa Palmata*, which in subsequent years of wartime neglect covered the whole area in an impenetrable jungle, and so it remains today. The other major project was more successful in its outcome though melancholy in its origin. Eleanor had a riding accident and for the last fifty or so years of her life was semi-crippled. The old greenhouse near the drawing room (which Minnie had described in 1880 as 'almost fallen down') was removed and replaced by a small Lutyensesque summerhouse. A new greenhouse, 150 feet long, was ordered in 1900 from Skinner Board & Co. Ltd. of Bristol, and erected against the outside south wall of the hidden garden; the price, on a 'supply and fix' basis, was £380. Two of the five sections were paved with quarry tiles and made generally convenient for the lady of the house in her Bath chair. Its convex shape and wire tension construction, with no external timber or paintwork, made the new greenhouse both elegant and durable and, with one overhaul after eighty years, it remains in fine shape today, as does the summerhouse.

Above: Glasshouse, 2007.

J.I.D. died in 1935, and the next generation was his son Robert (Bob) and his wife Helena. They had scarcely time to become installed before the start of World War II. The house became a home for convalescent servicemen. The kitchen garden flourished and expanded as the demand for its produce increased, but the rest of the gardens, particularly the outlying parts, inevitably went into a regime of, at best, minimum maintenance – despite welcome help given by high-ranking German officers from the nearby P.O.W. camp, including the construction of a rose pergola. Recovery after the war was not helped by the fact that Bob became an invalid, and it was a considerable achievement to regain and maintain control of the immediate lawns and beds and to have created (Helen's particular joy) a herbaceous border on the lower terrace.

Their daughter, Jenny, and I moved into Merthyr Mawr from Oxford in 1966. The labour force was now three, but was shortly reduced to one gardener, whose main responsibility was the kitchen garden and greenhouses. Our ambition was to push back to the pre-war frontiers, with the aid of more modern machinery and (be it confessed) chemicals more efficient than the

Above: Aerial view of Merthyr Mawr House, 1947.

sulphur and 'quarter-pound of tobacco' which in 1822 was required 'for the gardener for the use of the Hot House'. The bamboo garden defeated us, *Sasa Palmata* soon showing its ability to shrug off both chemical warfare and its own flowering. Elsewhere, however, the gardens were brought back. Such gravel paths as had survived the war were largely eliminated, with the exception of one converted into a sinuous gravel river for plants appreciating dry conditions. Lawns lost their mowing stripes and the kitchen garden became less productive (and more ornamental). The rockery near the terraces had already gone, but we also eliminated the tank garden (nothing is as inimical to water features as having vulnerable toddlers about; we eventually created a small pond nearby – on which the present generation is now looking askance!).

This process of simplification involved some losses, but we consoled ourselves with the reflection that much of what was lost was the 'public parks' atmosphere, and public parks were (were they not?) by definition vulgar. Sour grapes of course! We also flattered ourselves that the gains outweighed the losses; a landscaped swimming pool garden was created, the woodland gardens around the chapel and elsewhere were restored and extended, modest arboreta planted, and having inherited seven magnolias of various species, we left for posterity forty-three – all flourishing. Many of these endeavours had been made considerably easier by the virtual disappearance of the rabbit population following myxomatosis.

SOUTH WEST VIEW OF
MERTHYR MAWR HOUSE
1973

The present generation took over in 2005, and though mainly preoccupied with the house, has also begun to lay its imprint on the gardens. It will no doubt add, change and take away, as have all its predecessors, but what will remain is Sir John's conception. If he were to return, I believe that he would, on the whole, be pleased, certainly by his tree plantings (though he should hurry if he wishes to catch his magnificent beeches which are reaching the end of their lives). He would be pleased, too, by the survival of a landscape progression, almost seamless in space and time southward and westward from his house – through gardens, pleasure grounds, park, village, woodland, to the great sandhills where man has been since Mesolithic times, and at last to the sea. To the east, by contrast, the A48 trunk road is a very palpable seam, and the transition to Bridgend and modern life far more abrupt. Meanwhile we look forward to the next two hundred years.

Murray A. McLaggan

Below: South front of house, 1990.

Above: Remains of the ha-ha. 2005.

Left: Steps and topiaried yews on edge of south lawn, 2005.

House and gardens underwent considerable changes in the twentieth century. The house was gutted by fire in 1922 and rebuilt. During the Second World War it was requisitioned as a military convalescent hospital and for some years after the war functioned as a civilian hospital. Having been handed back to the family, the house was again ravaged by fire in the 1950s after which it was restored and converted into flats by the then owner Juliette, Lady Rhys Williams. Her son, Sir Brandon Rhys Williams sold the house in 1985 when it was converted into a hotel, a role which it fulfils to the present day. The development of the hotel has led to changes in the garden, few of which have significantly altered their essential layout or content. Both in terms of planting and maintenance, Miskin survives as an Edwardian garden overlaid but not subsumed by more recent aesthetic and practical considerations.

Hilary M. Thomas

Right: Sir Rhys Rhys Williams with family and friends outside the summerhouse (by kind permission of Lady Rhys Williams).

Hotel and leisure complex in private ownership.
Walled kitchen garden in separate private ownership No public rights of access.

Sources

Primary
Memorandum, account and copy letterbook, 1774-77 (GRO D/DXge 24/4).
Information supplied to the author by Caroline Lady Rhys Williams.

Secondary
Cardiff Times, 13 May 1911.
Taliesin Morgan, *The History of Llantrisant* (Cardiff, 1898).
Dillwyn Lewis, *The History of Llantrisant* (Risca, 1975).
J. Barry Davies & others, *Pontyclun and Talygarn: a History & Topography* (Llantrisant & District History Society, 2002).

See also: Cadw/ICOMOS; Newman; Royal Commission, *The Greater Houses.*

Nash Manor, Llysworney

N ash Manor lies approximately half a mile south of Llysworney village and a few miles south-west of Cowbridge. The house which stands today bears witness to many centuries of occupation. Its architecture incorporates features from the sixteenth century to the present day and it is one of the finest and architecturally most intriguing 'sub-medieval' houses in Glamorgan.

Below: East façade of house and lawn, 2006.

The house stands in the former extra-parochial district of Nash, once a possession of the medieval bishops of Llandaff, and until the 1960s the remains of the medieval chapel of St Osmund stood to the east of the house. By the 1430s the Carne family, in the person of Howell Carne, was established at Nash which remained the home of generations of Carnes for another four centuries. Howell and his successors augmented their estates in the Vale of Glamorgan by marriage and by purchase, and by the sixteenth century were prominent members of Glamorgan's gentry, wealthy, powerful and prominent in the official life of the county. Roger Carne of Nash was the first clerk of the peace of Glamorgan in 1539 and the family provided a number of sheriffs of the county in the sixteenth and seventeenth centuries. A younger son of Nash, Sir Edward Carne, who was to establish himself at Ewenny after the dissolution of the monasteries, rose to great eminence in legal and diplomatic circles.

Above: Nash Manor, watercolour by Charlotte Louisa Traherne, c1850 (by kind permisssion of the McLaggan family).

Of the gardens which surrounded Nash in the first centuries of Carne ownership virtually nothing is known, although it must be supposed that the status and wealth of the family would have ensured suitably fashionable gardens to complement their residence. All that can be said with certainty is that by the 1530s a park for fallow deer had been established at Nash, a fact recorded by the antiquary John Leland, and that the park still survived at the end of the sixteenth century when it was noted by Rice Merrick and Rice Lewis. Today, the north-west boundary of that park can still be identified in woodland bordering the entrance drive to Nash Manor.

Not until the eighteenth century does a picture of the gardens at Nash begin to appear. The diaries of the Reverend John Carne run from 1763-98, and in his jottings for 1785 Carne provides some useful information regarding work on house and garden. He writes that his grandfather Edward Carne built the stable north of the house, his grandmother the little parlour adjoining the house, his father the little barn and he himself the garden walls, greenhouse and pigeon house. Other diary entries of the reverend gentleman reveal that he planted mulberry trees in the 1760s and that in 1771 he obtained a White Bury Standard Pear from Bristol and planted it in the east circle of the garden. Occasional references to vegetables including cucumbers, suggest a productive kitchen garden. It would be foolish to read too much into these sparse records, but they do suggest that the Reverend John Carne's enthusiasm for gardens had not been shared by his immediate predecessors at Nash and that he was, if not creating a new garden at Nash, improving its design and content.

The aerial photograph of Nash dating from just before the Second World War reveals a formal pattern of hedged and walled enclosures, all in immaculate order, a pattern which tempts the hypothesis that here is encapsulated the design of a garden whose origins reach back to the seventeenth century if not earlier. It shows a walled rectangular enclosure, extending eastwards from the east wing of the house, with a central path bisecting it along its length. On either side of this path are rectangular, hedged and grassed enclosures of varying size, everything running in uncompromisingly straight lines. The perimeter walls and the glasshouses on the south face of the north wall are presumed to be those built by the Reverend John Carne in the late eighteenth century, but the strict formality (still apparent in the mid twentieth century) within those walls does raise the possibility that the walls replaced earlier hedges and fences. And immediately in front of the east wing the same photograph shows the pattern of a 'knot garden' bordered with box, a feature already well established in the 1860s when a photograph shows it maintained in good order.

South of the main garden enclosure, the same aerial photograph reveals several 'compartments', two of which were probably created in Victorian and Edwardian times. One, with a central path running east to west between neatly trimmed yews and borders is now known as The Victorian Walk. South of this is a sunken area laid out in the pattern and patriotic design of a Union Jack. Today, vestiges of the Victorian Walk still survive as does the low stone wall and steps leading into the sunken area, but all traces of the Union Jack layout have long vanished and the enclosure is now grassed. However, family photographs of the Nicholl Carne family and reminiscences of a present-day descendant of the family reveal that the Union Jack garden was laid out with rose bushes some time before the First World War and that it was probably the inspiration of Mrs Alice Annie Nicholl Carne, a keen gardener, who had moved into Nash with her husband John Van Loder Nicholl Carne in the 1880s and who remained in residence there until her death in 1931. The recollections of a housekeeper at Nash after the departure of the Nicholl Carnes suggest that the Union Jack garden later became a 'vegetable parterre'. On the eastern side of this former garden there survive some mature rhododendrons which were introduced in the nineteenth century and are remarkably vigorous survivors in a limestone region. In the same area a line of ancient yews may indicate a former yew tunnel.

Right: Steps and urns, photograph by Edwin Miles, early C20th (Glamorgan Record Office).

Right:
Gatehouse, 2005.

Photographs taken in the first half of the twentieth century show the gardens at Nash as they were when the last generations of the Nicholl Carne family were still in residence. A conservatory standing against the east façade of the house was pulled down and replaced by a sunken garden, again the work of Alice Nicholl Carne. The walls of the north gatehouse and courtyard in the 1920s and 1930s were covered with climbing plants (including wisteria and roses), while the central path leading to the entrance door was lined with tubs of agapanthus. Lawns are shown neatly mown, shrubs and climbers against the house neatly trimmed. After the building of the new west wing of the house in the late nineteenth century, the wing which included the children's nursery, the little lawn immediately to the right of the north porch was known as the Nursery Lawn.

Above:
Thomas and Eric Tebby, gardeners at Nash c.1950 (by kind permission of Jennifer & Eric Williams).

In c.1950 Mrs Isabel Nicholl Carne moved from Nash to Great House, Llanblethian, Nash was sold and the long connection of the Carnes with Nash Manor came to an end. Another connection ended in December 1957 with the death of Thomas Tebby who had been head gardener at Nash Manor for over sixty-five years. When he took up his appointment in 1890 he is reported to have had twenty-one men working under him; in his latter years most of the work was done entirely by him and his son Eric.

Below: Estate workers, early C20th.

In the half century and more since the aerial photograph was taken, the gardens at Nash Manor have undergone many changes. Much of the main

walled enclosure is now a single lawned area with a rectangular fishpond centrally sited. A conifer hedge on its south side gives access to a pleasant gravelled courtyard (recently created from a previously grassed court) from which 'original' ornamental iron gates lead towards the south lawn and Victorian Walk. Beyond the lawn are the skeletal remains of the once extensive and productive glasshouses which stood against the south-facing wall.

Above: Pond and yew hedge, 2006.

Above: Ornamental ironwork.

Above: View across the terraces, 2006.

Below: Summerhouse, 2006.

Below: The castle above the terraces, 2006.

At the southern extremity of the terraces a triangular slope leads down to a terrace walk above a lawn overlooking the Cavalry Barracks, a stone structure built in the late sixteenth or early seventeenth century probably as stables. This area of the gardens was known in the Edwardian period as the Harp Garden and is believed to have been created in that form by Dr J. W. Nicholl Carne.

Some areas of garden beyond the terraces were also part of the Tudor design. West of the castle, at the foot of the east side of the valley, are two long parallel grass terraces running south from the churchyard and separated from each other by a stone wall with three rounded projections. These terraces, thought to date from the time of Sir Edward Stradling, are connected by an arched opening which gives access from the upper to the lower terrace from which a flight of stone steps leads to the valley floor.

Below: The grass walk with the double walls, 2006.

The 'spacious level area luxuriant with grass … between two groves' described in a poem by Sir Edward's kinsman and heir Sir John Stradling is little changed today, with the eye being led across the valley to the remains of a Watch Tower, a stone structure probably built as a lookout in the fifteenth century and a feature of the sixteenth/seventeenth century landscape.

Above: Wisteria on steps, 2006.

In scale, splendour and sophistication the gardens at St Donats were rivalled in south Wales only by those at Raglan in Monmouthshire. Sir Edward's travels in Italy and his familiarity with classical architecture and literature clearly influenced his overall concept for the gardens at St Donats, a concept, which, when realised, must have mightily impressed all visitors to the castle. Poets, among them Thomas Leyshon and Sir John Stradling, were inspired to compose long poems, full of classical and allegorical allusions, heaping praise upon the gardens and their creator. Of particular interest in these poems are the references to plants cultivated in Sir Edward's gardens, plants such as the 'juicy vine' [fig tree?] mentioned by John Stradling, and the 'sweet fruits of the vines, nards [spike lavender], amomum [winter cherry], roses and beautiful lilies' praised by Thomas Leyshon. Despite the proximity of the castle to the sea and its exposure to the full force of the prevailing winds, the sheltering walls of the gardens enabled a wide variety of plants, including tender species, to be grown. Essentially Italianate in inspiration and design Sir Edward's garden, described in Thomas Leyshon's poem as many-hued and shining with many beautiful flowers to feast the eye, may also have contained marble and polished stones brought from Italy and used to make 'columns of wonderful material … glowing beyond measure for their art', as described by Sir John Stradling.

Below: The Tudor Garden with king's beasts, 2006.

Above: The Rose Garden, 2006.

Sir Edward Stradling was the epitome of the wealthy Renaissance man. Oxford educated, trained in the law, he was a prominent figure in local justice and administration, and also served the Crown on special commissions. Respected by many of his learned contemporaries and described by his friend William Camden as 'vir doctissimus' [most learned of men], he was a patron of Welsh poets and harpists and had 'a singular knowledge of the British [Welsh] language and antiquities'. Stradling's magnificent library at St Donats with its priceless collection of books and manuscripts reflected his wide-ranging interests and accomplishments and made the castle a centre of learning and culture. It was equally a place of generous and lavish hospitality. And the magnificent gardens set the castle within an appropriately sophisticated setting and reflected the status of this wealthy, cultured man. They were gardens on which visitors gazed with awed amazement, gardens which inspired poets to lavish effusions of praise, gardens which overwhelmed the senses and stimulated the intellect. The gardens have survived, virtually intact, to the present day. They are a wonderful legacy which, in the words of Elisabeth Whittle, inspector of historic parks and gardens for Cadw, 'should take their rightful place in the pantheon of the greatest surviving Tudor gardens in Britain'.

Hilary M. Thomas

Right: A king's beast.

*Home of Atlantic College. Gardens and castle open to the
public on occasional days in the year, as advertised.*

Sources

Primary
Map of St Donat's estate, by W.J. Rees, 1862 (GRO, D/D AbD).
St Donats tithe award, 1843 (GRO).

Secondary
Roy Denning (ed.), *The Story of St Donat's Castle and Atlantic College* (1983).
Jeston Homfray, *The Castles of the Lordship of Glamorgan* (Cardiff, 1828).
G.T. Clark , *Thirteen Views of the Castle of St Donat's* (Shrewsbury, 1871).
H. Avray Tipping, 'St Donat's Castle, Glamorganshire', *Country Life*, XXII (24 and 31 August 1907).
Elisabeth Whittle,'The Tudor Gardens of St Donat's', *Garden History*, 27.1 (1999).
Cardiff Times, 6 Novemeber 1909.

See also: Cadw/ICOMOS; Grose; Royal Commission, *The Later Castles.*

St Fagans Castle, St Fagans

The Elizabethan mansion house, St Fagans Castle, dominates the skyline on the approach to St Fagans village from the south, standing as it does on the lip of a steep slope which drops down to the valley of the river Ely. This strategically defensive position harks back to the medieval period and to the first castle built on the site in the twelfth century, but the earliest known gardens at St Fagans coincide with the building of 'a very faire house' on the ruins of the medieval structure towards the end of the sixteenth century.

Having passed through a succession of owners in the medieval period, the castle, together with its lands forming the St Fagans estate, was purchased in the 1560s by a Dr John Gibbon and it is he, or his immediate successor Nicholas Herbert, who is credited with building the new mansion and starting on the creation of a garden landscape around the house. In 1616 St Fagans was purchased by Edward Lewis of The Van, Caerphilly, who lavished considerable sums of money on the interior embellishment of the castle and can be assumed to have continued the enhancement of the gardens. St Fagans remained in the possession of the Lewis family until 1730 when the heiress Elizabeth Lewis married Other, 3rd Earl of Plymouth, thereby uniting her family's extensive Glamorgan estates with those of the Plymouth/Windsor family. The Lewises, in their century of ownership of St Fagans, had spent little time at the castle, preferring to reside at The Van and later on their Soberton (Hampshire) estates. The principal residence of the earls of Plymouth was the family seat at Hewell Grange, near Bromsgrove in the Midlands, and for successive generations of the family residence at St Fagans was never more than occasional and brief. Not until the 1850s did St Fagans take a more central place in the life of the Windsor/Plymouth family, and it was then that the castle was refurbished and the gardens transformed into 'one of the most important historic gardens in Wales'.

But the origins of the gardens at St Fagans, as already indicated, can be traced back to the age of the Tudors, if not earlier, and what can be seen at St Fagans today is a palimpsest of garden history where the strong impact of nineteenth- and early twentieth-century design has obscured but not totally effaced the patterns of earlier centuries.

Right: Detail from St Fagans estate map showing house and gardens, 1766 (Glamorgan Record Office).

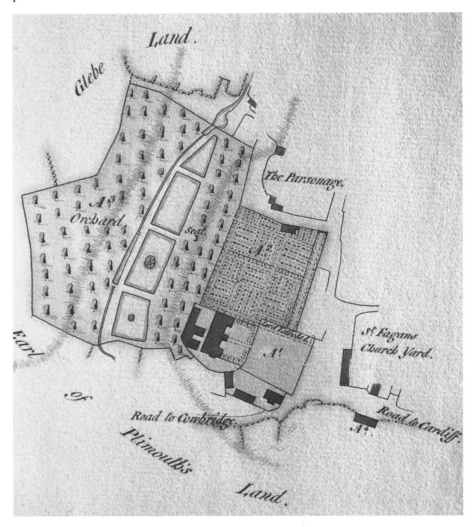

Above: Aerial view of St Fagans Castle, 1930 (Cardiff Central Library).

During and in the immediate aftermath of the Second World War, when labour was scarce, the gardens could not be maintained to the standards of their heyday and economies had to be made. Much of the topiary, until then such a dominant feature of the gardens, disappeared, simpler planting schemes were introduced and some of the formal designs within the compartment gardens were modified. Since 1946, when the Earl of Plymouth gave St Fagans to the National Museum of Wales (later the National Museum and Gallery of Wales and now National Museum Wales) for the establishment of the Welsh Folk Museum (later the Museum of Welsh Life and now St Fagans: National History Museum) much of the wider parkland and woodland surrounding the castle has been transformed into the open air museum.

*Above: Topiary on the
north side of the house,
1940s.*

*Below: Topiary, 1950
(by kind permission of
Sylvia Crawshay).*

Above: The Goscombe John statue 'The Elf', 1950 (by kind permission of Sylvia Crawshay).

Below: 'The Elf' and 'Joyaunce', now located on island in the water garden, 2004.

Above: Knot garden, 2004.

A *Handbook* published by the Museum in 1953, while devoted mainly to the castle and its contents and to buildings being re-erected in the grounds, also drew attention to the gardens, in particular the Fountain Garden, the Rose Garden and Mulberry Grove to the north of the house, and the finely-wrought iron gates at the entrance to the Rose Garden leading to the bronze figure of *Joyance* by Sir William Goscombe John RA. Another Goscombe John bronze, *The Elf*, stood north of the fishponds in the Water Garden below the castle. In 1998 *Joyance* was placed on a pedestal in the new Rosery, but in 2003 was relocated to the Water Garden where it now stands in the same area as *The Elf*. Glasshouses in the Mulberry Grove survive to the present day, but they have long ceased to produce the 'grapes available for purchase' of the 1950s.

*Above: The Italian
Garden, 2004.*

*Right: Doorway into
the Italian Garden.*

*Far Right: The Italian
Garden, agapanthus
reflected in water.*

Above: Porch, Old Beaupre.

heyday, only faint traces can still be discerned in the sloping fields around the house and identified within the walled courtyards. On the east side of the middle courtyard a raised grass terrace backs onto the curtain wall which originally had a wall walk along the top providing a view across the deer park. It is thought that the inner courtyard was probably partly, if not entirely, devoted to garden. On the west wall of the enclosure which is now the garden of the farmhouse there survives evidence of a small building which projected over the slope providing a look-out across the terraces below. Beyond the house to the north-east, where vestiges of walls, banks and ditches survive, another area of garden led down the sloping ground towards the river Thaw and to a series of ponds along the river, ponds now barely identifiable in a series of turfed depressions.

The Manor

Within the village, The Manor and Village Farm are among the more substantial surviving houses with proven sixteenth-century pedigrees, but it is not until the eighteenth and nineteenth centuries that details of their gardens are revealed. The Manor (also called The Great House) was home to members of the Edmondes family in the late eighteenth century and subsequently passed by marriage to the Traherne family. The house was substantially altered c.1800 and it is probable that the garden landscape which endured throughout the nineteenth and much of the twentieth century was created at this time. Lawns and the ha-ha on the south side of the house still survive from this earlier period, but the extensive pleasure gardens to the west, as shown on the 1877 Ordnance Survey map and in later photographs, have been eroded by the building in the 1960s of a new house (and the creation of a delightful garden) within the site.

Above: The Manor House, 1913.

In 1913 The Manor, then in possession of the Saunderson family as legatees of the Trahernes, was sold at auction. The sale catalogue of this date gives a detailed picture of the gardens, emphasising not only the picturesque setting of the house but also the more utilitarian resources of the kitchen garden:

> *The garden has a beautiful warm wall the entire length of the Western side and is well stocked with Fruit Trees and Fruit Bushes. The Lawns and Flower Gardens are tastefully laid out and well shaded by many fine old trees, the whole forming a most attractive, picturesque country Residence.*

The kitchen garden with its grass and box edged paths contained a large greenhouse and tomato house, a lean-to vinery, cucumber frames, a thatched tool house and a wooden tool house. Well removed from the house and gardens was a cow shed with two ties and two pig cots – evidently horticulture and animal husbandry were complementary activities at The Manor. A photograph included in the sale catalogue shows neatly trimmed lawns and flower beds on the west and south sides of the house. A photograph taken some forty years later shows the wider gardens of The Manor, all still in immaculate order, with the western walled area laid out in a variety of geometrically shaped beds to fit the irregular shape of the site.

Above: Village Farm, 1997.

Village Farm

Village Farm was the largest farm in the village. In a reconstruction drawing of the house in its sixteenth-century form by RCAHMW a simple walled forecourt garden is indicated on the south entrance front of the property with two paved and parallel paths leading to the main entrances. Low hedges and small beds, the latter containing a mixture of herbs, other flowering plants and vegetables for culinary and medicinal use, would probably have been incorporated into this enclosure. In subsequent centuries the garden was extended beyond the confines of the walled forecourt and the 1877 Ordnance Survey map clearly shows its extent and layout and indicates a little of its content with the whole area bisected along its length by a central path, cross paths edged with trees and bushes, and formal rectangular beds. The latter features can be presumed to have endured from the sixteenth century. The tennis court at the far end of the garden was probably laid out in the early years of the twentieth century, its creation indicative of a certain social status held by the Village Farm family within the community. In a photograph of the 1950s the garden looks neglected and this impression is corroborated by the recollections of a descendant of the family then living in Village Farm who believes that the garden was kept in good trim up to the Second World War. His childhood recollections of the years before 1947, when the tenancy of the farm passed to another family, is of the vast garden going to ruin, the paths overgrown, the box hedges neglected and the tennis court abandoned. Much of the garden, he thinks, was ploughed up at that time. The same person recalls that the paved area in front of the farmhouse, called the bailey, had a low wall on the south side beyond which was a lawn.

Above: The Cottage, photograph by Edwin Miles, early C20th (Glamorgan Record Office).

The Cottage

The value of sale catalogues in the context of garden history is also illustrated in another St Hilary property, The Cottage, not a cottage at all but an elegant Regency-style villa built in the first half of the nineteenth century for the Reverend George Traherne, vicar of St Hilary from 1832 to 1853. The villa incorporated within its structure an older, more modest 'cottage-like' property of whose garden nothing is known, but it is likely that it was the reverend gentleman who was responsible for laying out the lawns, shrubberies and rock gardens referred to in a sale catalogue of 1939 and in planting the shelter belt on the north side of the grounds. The layout of the kitchen garden is clearly shown on the 1877 Ordnance Survey map which also shows a sizeable

Below: Aerial View of St Hilary, c.1950.

glasshouse structure against the north wall suggesting that this too was part of the Reverend George Traherne's creation of The Cottage gardens. The 1939 sale catalogue itemises two large vineries, a lean-to vinery and three forcing houses within the kitchen garden, all described as heated but in a poor state of repair, and the map accompanying the catalogue shows at least two new glasshouses intruding into the central area of the kitchen garden when compared with the 1877 map.

Above: Cottages, 1913.

Village Cottages

The gardens attached to the small, often thatched cottages in the village – Myrtle, Manor and the others – were of an altogether different order from those of their superior namesake. For most of the tenants of the cottages the garden was an essential provider of food for the family, a vital supplement to the household's income. Photographs of the late-nineteenth and early-twentieth centuries show front gardens stocked with profusions of vegetables and fruit bushes, but space was invariably found for flowers and few cottage walls were unadorned with climbing roses or ornamental creepers. One property in the village whose garden still evokes the cottage garden of earlier centuries is The Old Post Office where a central path leads from the front gate through the walled garden with its lawns and fruit trees (but no vegetables) to the front door. In the 1860s, annual Cottagers' Exhibitions for parishes in the immediate vicinity of Cowbridge were held to encourage and reward the cottage gardeners. Instituted by some twenty-two local gentlemen, a certain combination of paternalism and encouragement of the work ethic is detectable in the stated objectives of the event:

The competition is limited to the labouring class and no obstacle is placed in the way of the humblest cottager if he feels disposed to make an exertion in the cultivation of flowers and vegetables.

The 1866 exhibition was held at St Quentin's Castle, Llanblethian, under banners which read 'Success to the Cottage Garden Exhibition' and 'The hand of the diligent maketh rich', and on this occasion it was the vegetables rather than the flowers of the cottagers, including those of St Hilary, that were adjudged worthy of prizes.

Old Beaupre apart, the 'historic' gardens of St Hilary are unexceptional in form and content and their documentation is scarce before the nineteenth century. What they do, in particular, is supplement our knowledge of the social composition and visual appearance of one Vale village in the Victorian and Edwardian period. The garden history of other Vale villages awaits exploration.

Hilary M. Thomas

Old Beaupre is in the care of Cadw and there is free public access via a footpath across farmland. All the village gardens are in private ownership and there is no public right of access to them.

Sources

Primary
Sale catalogues of estates in St Hilary, 1913, 1928 and 1939 (GRO D/D SA1, 12 and 14).

Secondary
Cardiff Times, 6 July 1912.
Hilary M. Thomas, *St Hilary: a History of the Place and its People* (St Hilary, 2000).
D.B .Hague, *Old Beaupre Castle, Glamorgan* (HMSO, 1965).
The Royal Commission on Ancient and Historical Monuments in Wales, *Inventory of Ancient Monuments in Glamorgan*, Vol.IV Part 2, *Farmhouses and Cottages* (1988).

See also: Cadw/ICOMOS; Merrick; Newman; Royal Commission, *The Greater Houses*.

Talygarn, Llantrisant

Talygarn Fawr, the 'great house' of Talygarn, is situated on elevated ground on the east side of the A4222 Llantrisant to Cowbridge road to the south of Pontyclun. It has a long history, and ownership of both house and lordship can be traced back to the fourteenth century. Some of the early owners probably had gardens of which no trace now remains, the first record of a garden at Talygarn being provided by the tithe map of 1841 when the then owner, Dr William Lisle, is shown to have had a garden together with orchards, plantations and a large meadow.

Dr William Berkin Meackham Lisle was the longest serving and largely absentee rector of St Fagans who had acquired Talygarn in about 1817 or 1818. He had bought it as a summer residence but was soon living there more or less permanently and farming on a large scale. Lisle was a tree enthusiast, and the plantations noted on the tithe map were probably his new plantings to protect his crops and vines from the easterly winds. He may also have planted some specimen trees, and possibly, but less certainly, the extensive orchards. He was an eccentric in many ways and local tradition has it that he was a poisons expert who kept a snakepit at Talygarn to house his deadly reptiles. The recent discovery of what may indeed have been a snakepit close to the house may confirm this, although Talygarn has always been known as a thriving area for grass snakes. By 1851 Lisle had moved back to St Fagans and both house and garden became neglected. After his death in 1856 Talygarn passed to his daughter Frances who sold it to George Clark in 1865.

Above: South lawn, photograph by Edwin Miles, early C20th (Glamorgan Record Office).

George Thomas Clark (1809-98) was an important Victorian ironmaster, engineer and scholar. At the time he acquired Talygarn he was living at Dowlais House, Merthyr Tydfil, as the resident trustee and manager of the Dowlais Iron Company. Talygarn was in poor condition and the major initial outlay made by Clark was on the land and on expensive farm buildings, although he did plant 'largely about the house, chiefly conifers and with great success for they grew wonderfully'. It was not until 1879 that major work on the house and gardens took place, and in that year Clark laid out the flower garden anew in two levels divided by a dwarf wall with two flights of steps. In a memoir, Clark mentions many of the improvements he made to the gardens. In 1893 a rose garden was created at the base of the water tower just east of the house and a platform made for tea drinking. The narrow North Lawn was widened and its stone balustrade fixed, and a little later the field beyond was excavated to a depth of about six feet and laid out as a square lawn with a central basin. To the south of the house and gardens a large ornamental lake was created.

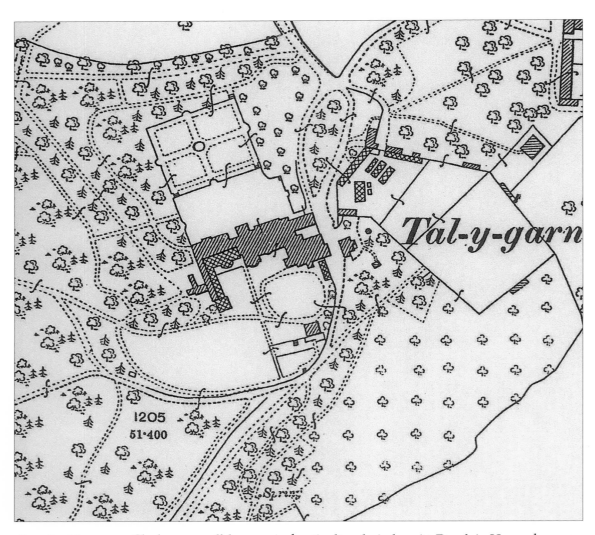

Above: Detail from first edition Ordnance Survey map, 1877.

Clark was well-known in horticultural circles. At Dowlais House he grew pineapples and at Talygarn vines and bananas. His garden and farm account books were meticulously kept and every detail recorded. He was elected to the Council of the Royal Horticultural Society in February 1876 and the following month became one of its vice-presidents.

In 1921 the Clark family decided to move permanently to London, and in 1923 Talygarn was sold to the South Wales Miners' Welfare Committee to become a convalescent home for mineworkers. The sale catalogue of that date evokes the splendour of the landscape created by Clark, describing the

house as being set

on an elevated position in the midst of exceedingly choice specimens of Ornamental Timber in association with delightfully Picturesque Grounds and Gardens containing beautiful examples of Flowering Shrubs all giving in their season a perfect wealth of bloom, the Lake below, nearly Eight Acres in extent bordered with Rhododendrons, affording from the South Front an enchanting view.

And the Rt. Hon. Thomas Richards, general secretary of the South Wales Miners' Federation recognised the value of Talygarn as a place for convalescence when he described the '140 acres of woodland, lawns, gardens, lakes, conservatories and shaded walks' with in every direction 'a prospect that is pleasing, beautiful and restful'. Talygarn subsequently became a miners' rehabilitation centre and later passed to the National Health Service. In March 2001 it was sold to developers who are currently converting the house to apartments and building new houses on sites formerly occupied by hospital buildings.

Below: North front and sunken garden, 2000.

Below: North front balustrading: (Patricia Moore).

Since the departure of the Clark family from Talygarn, house and gardens have undergone many changes but both would, in essence, still be recognisable to G.T. Clark. In front of the house on the north is a forecourt of lawn and tarmac bounded on the north by stone balustrading. This overlooks the sunken garden which is laid out to lawn with paths and a central stone-edged octagonal pool with fountain. The sunken garden is surrounded on three sides by mature ornamental trees and shrubs. In the centre of each of the perimeter paths on these three sides is a semi-circular alcove with a stone bench and paving in semi-circular pattern. To the east of the garden is an area of large shrubs divided by winding paths, still known locally as 'the maze'. From the north-east corner of the garden a flight of steps leads to a former north drive flanked by mature trees, among which are several huge sweet chestnuts thought to be more than two and a half centuries old and legacies of the pre-Clark era.

Above: Lead planter by Biraghi of Venice, 1894.

Below: Planter with Clark family motto 'Try and Trust'.

In each of the four corners of the sunken garden is a square, ornamental lead tub on a stone plinth. The tubs are decorated with diamond-pattern embossed friezes and heraldic devices incorporating the Clark family motto 'Try and Tryst' and the date '1893'. These tubs were designed by the Italian designer and carver Biraghi who was responsible for the wooden panelling and staircase within the house. Eight smaller lead tubs of similar design and dated '1894' originally surrounded the central pool but four were stolen some years ago and the remaining four are sited elsewhere in the garden. One large leaden basin similar to that of seventeenth-century date surviving at St Fagans Castle was 'chopped up' soon after the Second World War and sold as scrap.

In 1981 the health authority which then owned Talygarn decided to commemorate International Year of the Disabled by creating a garden for the disabled within the sunken area. Raised beds of differing heights were created within low stone walls and new diagonal paths were made.

The south front of the house looks out across a terrace to a level lawn with flower beds and two very fine specimen trees – a mature cedar of Lebanon (*Cedrus libani*) and a large cork oak (*Quercus suber*) said to be the finest of its kind in Wales. At the east end of the lawn is a projection which was the site of the former water tower, adjacent to which was the area described by Clark as a 'tea platform'. West of the house on this side was the conservatory known for many years as the Winter Garden and thought to be the building which Clark sometimes called the Myrtle House. Here he grew bananas and vines and no doubt other exotic plants. Old photographs show it to have been a single-storey glazed building with a central canted section, pitched glazed roof and with a two storey section at its east end. This conservatory was pulled down in 1951 having been declared dangerous. Against the nearby wall there survives a *Magnolia grandiflora*.

Above: South lawn, 2000.

Below: Rose Garden and terraces, 2000.

On the map of the demesne the castle is shown as a long, narrow building on its scarp-edged platform, with several associated buildings some of which are obviously stables. It is difficult, however, to interpret the ground plan of the house and we have no idea what it looked like. Immediately adjoining the castle to the north was a rectangular 'Green' which must be the bowling green mentioned in a letter of 1776. To the east of the main drive were the gardens, a nursery and a shrubbery with paths. The rectangular garden compartments consisted of a kitchen garden, a 'garden', (presumably a flower garden) with a formal layout around a central circular feature, a drying ground and a rickyard. Part of the stone wall that surrounded the gardens still stands. To the south of the kitchen garden was a broad, straight

Right: Wenvoe Castle, watercolour by Charlotte Louisa Traherne, c.1830 (by kind permisssion of the McLaggan family).

promenade, probably the continuation of a terrace in front of the castle and known as the Long Walk. Beyond the castle and gardens were three separate areas of parkland, named as 'Lawn' (nearly 62 acres), 'Waun Lawn' (nearly 17 acres) and 'Upper Lawn' (25 acres), the first two having a scattering of single trees and small groups of trees. Between the Lawn and the Upper Lawn was perhaps the most interesting feature then at Wenvoe, the intriguingly named 'Coed y Bear' (Bears Wood). In this wooded area of only 25 acres there were several round clearings linked together by serpentine walks or rides. In a northern projection of Bears Wood was a sinuous canal, formed by damming the Brynhill brook, and a grotto. Traces of these features survive in a ruinous state. Around the outer perimeter of the grounds there is evidence for the planting of belts of trees; along the Port Road, the southern boundary, was a 'nursery of fir'.

It is worth noting a building on the estate beyond the demesne. On the high ground of the Downs, alongside the turnpike road from Cardiff to Cowbridge, one of William Morrice's maps shows what the local diarist William Thomas liked to call a 'folly'. Usually known as the summerhouse, and approached from Wenvoe Castle along a two-mile carriageway, the building took the form of a Gothic castle with two towers. It afforded panoramic views in every direction, across the estate, the Vale and the Bristol Channel.

Although the Wenvoe Castle demesne in 1762 amounted to only 141 acres, and so was on a rather modest scale, there is every sign that Sir Edmund Thomas had been at work to create stylish surroundings for his perhaps old-fashioned house. He continued to enlarge and improve the grounds for the remaining five years of his life. The question is, how much of what is visible on the maps was the work of Sir Edmund since his coming of age in 1733? It was almost certainly he who built the summerhouse on the Downs, but it is more difficult to assess his role in the demesne. The Cadw/ICOMOS *Register* argues on stylistic grounds that the Green, the formal gardens and the Long Walk are likely to be older than Sir Edmund's tenure of the estate. The shrubbery and Bears Wood, with their circuits of paths or rides, are considered to be in the rococo style of the 1730s to 1750s, transitional between the earlier geometric formality of garden design and the naturalistic landscape garden fashionable in the 1760s. The creation of the landscaped park was probably begun by Sir Edmund before 1762 and was further developed by him up to 1767. The extension of the park required the purchase of adjoining land and the closure or realignment of several roads. In the sale catalogue of 1769 the demesne was 273 acres, substantially more than in 1762. An account of Sir Edmund's life, written at the time of his sudden death in 1767 by the diarist William Thomas, gives a local perspective on the baronet's activities:

> He had much delight in cleaning the land about his palace, in planting clumps of fir, in changing lanes and pulling down houses and build[ing] some ... On his way in his thoughts to pull down all the houses at Burden's Hill, and to make a park about his house etc.

A sophisticated traveller of 1769, the Hon. James Grimston, thought that the grounds around Wenvoe Castle 'by being laid out in the modern taste, are rather pleasing, and show the genius of the father of the present possessor'. There is no hint in any known record that Sir Edmund employed a landscape gardener at Wenvoe. He would have found his inspiration in the many

Above: Wenvoe Castle (south front), c.1910.

gardens he had seen on visits to the country estates of his relatives and friends in fashionable parts of England.

Grimston went on to record that the late baronet 'fired with the zeal of electioneering and improving his place, spent here more than the income of his estate would allow' and that his son was 'obliged to pay off the debts his father contracted by parting with his inheritance', and William Thomas confirms that Sir Edmund had died 'in debt with all sort'. It was several years before a buyer for the estate could be found, but in 1775 Peter Birt, a native of Berkshire who had made his fortune in the Aire and Calder Navigation in Yorkshire, became the new owner. He paid £41,000 for the estate and, over the next sixteen years, bought more land to enlarge his original purchase from 3,750 acres to just under 5,000 acres, as shown on the second Wenvoe estate survey made by Thomas Morrice in 1798.

There is little evidence that Peter Birt made major changes to the grounds at Wenvoe, though it is at least possible that he was responsible for some of the alterations to be identified through a comparison of the 1762 and 1798 maps. Birt's great work at Wenvoe was the rebuilding of the castle. He must have

Above: Wenvoe Castle, c.1910.

been seriously contemplating a new house very soon after taking possession, for plans drawn up by Robert Adam, dated 2 April 1776, are extant and a series of letters from Thomas Roberts, the man in charge of the rebuilding, begins on 29 April 1776, by which time the foundations were almost all ready. The house, when completed in 1777 or 1778 was large – an immense front of 374 feet, having a central residential block flanked by low wings terminating in pavilions at either end, and the whole surmounted by battlements. From the north (the entrance front) the wings were invisible behind screens of shrubs. A little to the north-east, but connected to the main house by an open arcade, was the stable yard, believed to have been designed by Henry Holland, the son-in-law of Capability Brown. Brown and Holland were working for Lord Mountstuart at Cardiff Castle in 1777-8 and it was probably soon afterwards that the stables at Wenvoe were constructed. Whether or not Capability Brown was involved in the development of the landscape at Wenvoe is not known.

Peter Birt bequeathed the Wenvoe estate to his grandson, Robert Jenner, after whom several generations of Jenners succeeded. They modified the surroundings of the castle in many small ways, yet down to the 1930s the demesne remained very much what it had been at the death of Sir Edmund Thomas in 1767. Successive Ordnance Survey maps and numerous prints and photographs from the nineteenth and twentieth centuries show the vast south front of the castle largely covered in well-trimmed ivy and Virginia creeper, and that the terrace along the front of the house was lined on the one side with shrubs and a flower border and on the other, along the top of the slope, by an iron fence which kept at bay the sheep grazing the lawn below. At the east end of the terrace was a greenhouse with adjoining stove house and potting shed. There was a small conservatory opening out of the west end of the main corridor of the castle; both greenhouse and conservatory were probably mid-Victorian additions. On the steep slope to the west end of the castle was a rock garden, probably dating from Victorian or Edwardian times, the main man-made features of which can still be seen, albeit neglected and overgrown. At some time in the nineteenth century, changes were made to the walled gardens to the east of the castle; the two walled enclosures shown in 1762 were made into one and glasshouses were erected against the north wall. The drying yard and rickyard had disappeared from the scene. By the 1830s a new main drive to the castle had been laid out across Waun Lawn, but the lodge which stands at the entrance from the main road (the present A4050) was probably built later. It is shown on the Ordnance Survey map of the late 1870s.

Right: South front of surviving east pavilion and terrace, 2001.

The final period of prosperity for the Wenvoe estate was from the 1880s to the First World War. It had originally been entirely agricultural, but at the southern end of the estate the first dock at Barry was constructed between 1884 and 1889, and a railway carrying coal from the Rhondda and Rhymney valleys passed through Wenvoe on its way to Barry, where a town mushroomed, a considerable part of it built on land belonging to the Jenners. Mrs Laura Jenner was the owner of the estate during her widowhood from 1883 to 1926. An article in a local newspaper reported that Mrs Jenner took 'the warmest personal interest' in the gardens, and there is no doubt that both gardens and demesne reached the peak of their development in her time. In the early years of the twentieth century the Bothy was built close to the walled garden to provide accommodation for the gardeners.

Below: Golf course looking towards Bears Wood, 2001.

Following the death of Mrs Jenner, her nephew and heir, the Reverend Hugh Jenner, attempted to sell the castle and demesne, but no buyer could be found and in 1930 the greater part of the mansion was demolished. In 1936 a lease for 99 years was granted to the Wenvoe Castle Golf Club and today fairways and greens cover much of the former parkland. Bears Wood remains in private ownership.

Brian Ll. James

Above: Terrace where Wenvoe Castle once stood.

Wenvoe Castle Golf Club and land in private ownership.
No public right of access.

Sources

Primary
Wenvoe estate maps by William Morrice and Thomas Morrice, 1762-3 and 1798 (GRO D/D We E/1 and 2).
Wenvoe Estate sale catalogue, [1769] (GRO D/D Xqg).

Secondary
Cardiff Times, 22 October 1910.
Roy Denning, 'The Thomas family of Wenvoe, 1560-1800', in Stewart Williams (ed.), *The Garden of Wales* (Cowbridge, 1961).
Brian Ll. James, 'Contributions towards a history of Wenvoe Castle', *Transactions of the Cardiff Naturalists' Society,* XCVIII (1974-6).

See also: Cadw/ICOMOS; Lloyd; Newman; Royal Commission, *The Later Castles;* Hilary M. Thomas; William Thomas.

Bibliography

Cadw/ICOMOS, *Glamorgan: Register of Landscapes, Parks and Gardens of Special Historic Interest. Part I: Parks & Gardens* (Cadw, 2000).

Carlisle, Nicholas, *A Topographical Dictionary of the Dominion of Wales* (London, 1811).

Dunraven, Windham Thomas, 4th Earl of, *Past Times and Pastimes,* 2 vols. (London, 1922).

Dunraven, Windham Henry, 5th Earl of, *Dunraven Castle, Glamorgan: Some Notes on its History and Associations* (London, 1926).

Evans, C.J.O., *Glamorgan: its History and Topography* (Cardiff, 1938).

Gastineau, Henry, *Wales Illustrated in a Series of Views* (London, 1830).

Grose, Francis, 'Francis Grose's tour in Glamorgan, 1775', ed. T.J. Hopkins, *Glamorgan Historian,* Vol.1 (1963).

Leland, John, *The Itinerary in Wales of John Leland in or about the Years 1536 to 1539,* ed. Lucy Toulmin Smith (London, 1906).

Lewis, Samuel, *A Topographical Dictionary of Wales,* 2 vols. (London, 1833).

Lloyd, Thomas, *The Lost Houses of Wales,* Revised ed. (Save Britain's Heritage, 1989).

Malkin, Benjamin Heath, *The Scenery, Antiquities and Biography of South Wales* (London, 1804; 2nd ed.1807).

Merrick, Rice, *Morganiae Archaiographia: a Book of the Antiquities of Glamorganshire,* ed. Brian Ll. James (South Wales Record Society, 1983).

Moore, Donald (ed.), *Wales in the Eighteenth Century* (Swansea, 1976).
Newman, John, *The Buildings of Wales: Glamorgan* (London, 1995).

Nicholas, Thomas, *Annals and Antiquities of the Counties and County Families of Wales,* 2 vols. (London,1872).

Pierce,G.O., *Place-names in Glamorgan* (Cardiff, 2002).

Royal Commission on Ancient and Historical Monuments in Wales (Royal Commission on the Ancient and Historical Monuments of Wales), *An Inventory of the Ancient Monuments in Glamorgan: Vol. III, Medieval Secular Monuments. Part lb: The Later Castles from 1217 to the present (2000). Vol.III, Medieval Secular Monuments. Part II: Non-defensive (1982). Vol.IV, Domestic Architecture. Part I: The Greater Houses (1981).*

Spencer, Marianne Robertson, *Annals of South Glamorgan: Historical, Legendary, and Descriptive Chapters on some Leading Places of Interest* (Carmarthen, 1913).

Thomas, Hilary M., *A Catalogue of Glamorgan Estate Maps (Glamorgan Archive Service,* 1992).

Thomas, William, *The Diary of William Thomas of Michaelston-super-Ely ... 1762-1795,* ed. R.T.W. Denning (South Wales Record Society, 1995).

Whittle, Elisabeth, *The Historic Gardens of Wales* (Cadw, 1992).

Williams, Isaac J., *A Catalogue of Welsh Topographical Prints* (National Museum of Wales, 1926).

Wyndham, Henry Penruddocke, *A Tour through Monmouthshire and Wales,* 2nd ed. (Salisbury, 1781).

List of the Historic Gardens included in this publication giving National Grid Reference, Parish Location and Grade Status in the Cadw/ICOMOS Register.

NGR	GARDEN	GRADE
ST 010 781	Ash Hall, Ystradowen	–
ST 104 751	Coedarhydyglyn (Coedriglan), St George-super-Ely	II*
ST 120 760	The Court, St Fagans	
SS 98 74	Cowbridge, town gardens	
ST 095 808	Craig-y-parc, Pentyrch	II*
ST 143 732	Cwrtyrala, Michaelston-le-Pit	II
SS 955 685	Dimlands, Llantwit Major	
ST 095 723	Duffryn (Dyffryn), St Nicholas	I
SS 887 728	Dunraven Castle, St Brides Major	II
ST 047 680	Fonmon Castle, Penmark	II
SS 973 679	The Ham, Llantwit Major	
ST 047 798	Hensol Castle, Pendoylan	II
SS 98 74	Llanblethian, village gardens	
SS 994 729	Llandough Castle, Llandough-iuxta-Cowbridge	
SS 981 719	Llanmihangel Place, Llanmihangel	II*
ST 043 727	Llantrithyd Place, Llantrithyd	II*
SS 888 779	Merthyr Mawr House, Merthyr Mawr	II*
ST 056 802	Miskin Manor, Llantrisant	II
SS 962 729	Nash Manor, Llysworney	
SS 934 681	St Donats Castle, St Donats	I
ST 120 771	St Fagans Castle, St Fagans	I
ST 013 736 ST 009 720	St Hilary, Old Beaupre and village gardens,	II
ST 032 801	Talygarn, Llantrisant	II*
ST 121 713	Wenvoe Castle, Wenvoe	II

Index:

Welsh Historic Gardens Trust
Ymddiriedolaeth Gerddi Hanesyddol Cymru

This charitable trust was formed in 1989 to raise the profile of the historic parks and gardens of Wales and to play a role in their preservation and restoration. At that time, the future for gardens in Wales looked all too bleak. Many had fallen victim to insensitive planning, lack of money or sheer indifference. Today, things are very different. There is a great deal of interest in visiting gardens of all descriptions and learning about their history.

Our members come from all over Wales and beyond, linked by a common love of Welsh gardens and their history. Members in Wales belong automatically to their own County Branches and those across the borders to their nearest Branch in Wales, but all, wherever they live, are welcome to join in every aspect of the work of the Trust and to enjoy a varied and exciting programme of events including:

* Lectures, study days and garden visits
* Helping to carry out garden surveys
* Practical conservation work
* Researching the history of local gardens
* Monitoring planning applications
* Spreading awareness of the garden heritage of Wales.

For further information and latest news, see the WHGT website:
www.whgt.org.uk

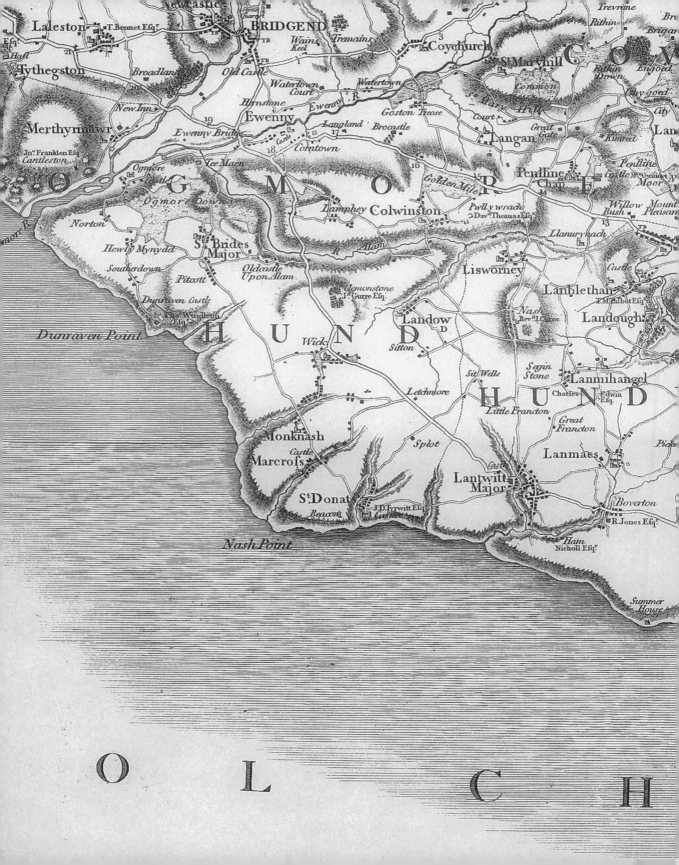